This book is dedicated to
Kathrine Kressmann Taylor

and to
my Gregory's Running Team mates:
Roger Adelman
Bill Glazier
Bob Hopple

and to
Louis Darden
wherever you are

Acknowledgments

To write this book about myself I needed more help than for any other. Considering the clarity of his memory, I think my old friend Roger Adelman ought to try his own hand at this. Contributions from my brother, Bill, and my mother were invaluable. What the three of us could not personally recall, I usually found in my father's meticulously compiled scrapbooks. Of great assistance also were Pete and Tina Pennock, Joe Mesi, Bill Steinberg, Millie Vircsik, Regina Simmonds, Ruth Riley, Bernice Foley, Carl Francis, Sandi Robinson, Judy Bitto, Larry Walker, Ellen Adams, my first editor John Keller, my agent and friend Ray Lincoln, and, as always, my wife, Eileen.

And Bill Hemsing, rifle-armed outfielder who stopped the ground balls that I missed and who hits the curve ball today better than ever.

For any inaccuracies contained in this account, I apologize. Where history could not be confirmed, it trembled at the mercy of my imperfect if well-meaning memory.

Knots in My Yo-yo String

The
Autobiography
of a Kid

by

Jerry Spinelli

E

EMBER

Visit us on the Web! randomhouse.com/kids

Educators and librarians, for a variety of teaching tools, visit us at randomhouse.com/teachers

The Library of Congress has cataloged the hardcover edition of this work as follows:
Spinelli, Jerry.
Knots in my yo-yo string : the autobiography of a kid / by Jerry Spinelli.
p. cm.
Summary: This Italian-American Newbery Medalist presents a humorous account of his childhood and youth in Norristown, Pennsylvania.
ISBN 978-0-679-98791-8 (lib. bdg.) — ISBN 978-0-307-48685-1 (ebook)
1. Spinelli, Jerry—Childhood and youth—Juvenile literature. 2. Authors, American—20th century—Biography—Juvenile literature. 3. Norristown (Pa.)—Social life and customs—Juvenile literature. 4. Italian Americans—Pennsylvania—Norristown—Biography—Juvenile literature.
[1. Spinelli, Jerry—Childhood and youth. 2. Authors, American. 3. Italian Americans.] I. Title
PS3569.P546Z47 1998
813'.54—dc21 97-30827

ISBN 978-0-679-88791-1 (pbk.)

Printed in the United States of America

35 34 33 32

First Ember Edition 2011
Random House Children's Books supports the First Amendment and celebrates the right to read.

Contents

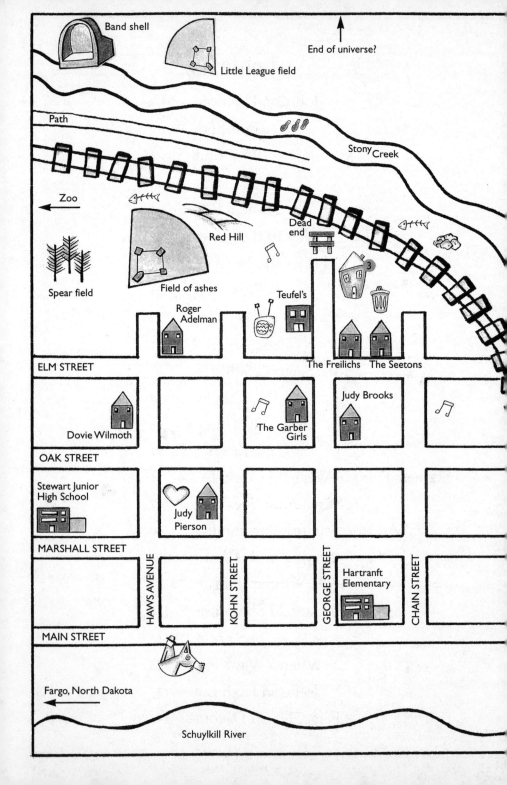

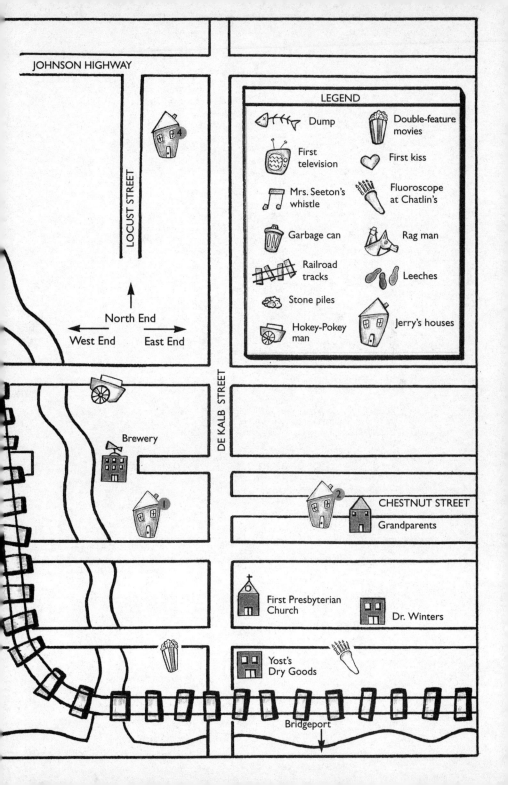

Johnson
Highway

Like much of my life until that sixteenth year, it was a sunny day. A Sunday afternoon. I was in Carol Eckert's house on Pine Street. We were in the living room. Carol was telling me about her new boyfriend, and I, as always, was the good listener.

The doorbell rang. It was my younger brother, Bill, panting. "Lucky was hit by a car!"

Lucky was our dog.

I didn't know what to say except, "Where?"

"Johnson Highway."

I apologized to Carol and left with Bill. We ran. We ran down Pine to Roberts, down Roberts to Locust, and up Locust toward Johnson Highway. As we came near, I wanted to say to Bill, "You look. I'm not stopping." I wanted to cross Johnson Highway and not look down but run on, run out of town, out of time, out of myself, because I was having a bad year, and it was too few hours ago that I was king.

East End

I am outside in the yard. There is the smell—sour, vaguely rotten. And then the sound. It is high-pitched, but that is not the problem. The radio makes high-pitched sounds, too, and so does my mother when she sings to me. The problem is the loudness, a force as feelable as a blizzard. Every morsel of me shrivels and shakes. And even so, maybe I could stand it if only it would stop. But it does not and does not—and I cannot hear my own scream. My mother is running out to get me...

This is my first memory of my first house. It was on Marshall Street in the so-called East End of Norristown, Pennsylvania. Behind the house was a brewery—the Adam Scheidt Brewing Company—and that, I later learned, was where the smell and the sound came from.

The smell was hops, used in the beer-brewing process. Forming a constant cloud about us, the odor was especially strong once a day when a horse-drawn wagon hauled spent mash down the alley that led from the brewery past our side yard. Then the alley became a sour, steaming stream from the drippings of the wagon's sopping cargo.

The source of the sound was an air-raid siren. It was propped on the roof of the brewery, hardly a stone's throw from our house. This was during the early 1940s. World War II was raging in Europe, Africa, and Asia, and air-raid drills were a common practice in towns and cities throughout the land.

While the siren's frightful wail seemed to come from everywhere, another frequent sound—a long, low drone—came from directly overhead. Many a day I looked up to see planes or airships—dozens, sometimes hundreds of them—moving in neat geometric shapes across the sky.

Our house was red brick, flanking a block-long row of red-brick houses that ended at the brewer's alley. The sidewalk was brick also. We lived in an apartment on the second floor. The Printzes—Mickey, Big Leroy, and Little Leroy—lived on the first floor. And on the third. Each night they trooped through our quarters to go up to bed.

The landlady lived in the adjoining house. Neighborhood kids said she was mean. Stray balls that landed in her yard never came out. Luckily for my father's baseball budget, she was nice to us. My father lobbed underhand pitches to me, and I regularly whacked them over the back fence into the landlady's yard. My father, according to Marshall Street lore, was the only person ever to return alive from her yard, ball in hand.

Unable to find a bat for a four-year-old, my father bought a standard-size Louisville Slugger, then put the saw to it. He presented me with seventeen inches of hickory handle—perfect. That stunted, clubbish "bat" stands in a corner of my office today. It reminds me of how small I once was, and that the landlady's fence was both the first and last fence that I ever hit a baseball over.

A budding ballplayer (age 4, 1945).

Over the fence out front, I sent something else. The gate facing the sidewalk was metal, and I used to grip those bars with my tiny hands and plant my feet and belt out "Jesus Loves Me" to the turning, smiling passersby.

At some point during my brief singing phase, I acquired a baby brother, Billy. My mother tells me that because I then had to compete for her attention, I brought my performances inside to the living room and kitchen.

*　　*　　*

The next house we lived in we had all to ourselves. It was also a row house, but it had a front porch. It was deeper into the East End, on Chestnut Street. I always remember the number—224 Chestnut—because my grandparents lived at 226, the house next door.

I wasn't allowed to cross the street. But I did roam up and down the sidewalk, and that led me to the vacant lot at the end of our row of houses. When I think of that lot, I think of weeds and of brown and blue broken glass. It became my first playground, my first ballfield. Many of my days were spent there, until I began school.

I did not go to kindergarten, so my first taste of school was first grade at Gotwals Elementary. We learned to write the letters of the alphabet, then our names. I recall laboring over each pencil-printed letter, and the miracle of completing my name on the blue-lined paper: my first written work.

I was destined to learn little else at Gotwals. We rented our house on Chestnut Street, but my parents had been searching for a place to buy. When they got the chance, they took it, even though it meant transferring me to a new first grade in a new school.

We were moving to the West End.

West
End

The West End became more than my home and neighborhood. It became my New World. No coonskin pathfinder ever explored his patch of earth more thoroughly than I explored mine.

The address was 802 George Street, second house in from Elm. Another brick row house, another brick sidewalk. For ten years I would live there, from ages six to sixteen.

The 800 block was the last block on George Street. It was a dead end. Beyond the last house the asphalt stopped. A three-foot-high wooden barrier made it official. I learned that "dead end" meant two different things. To a grownup it meant Stop—Turn the Car Around. To me, a kid, it meant Go—Your Territory Starts Here. Before the wooden barrier was the structured, orderly world of grownups, the neat grid of streets and houses that gave shape to their lives. Civilization.

Past the barrier was frontier. Climb over the fence or simply walk around it, as a car could not, and you found yourself in knee-high weeds. Then came the railroad tracks, then the woods, then the creek (pronounced "crick" in Norristown). This swatch of undeveloped land featured not one but two dumps, plus a swamp, Red Hill, the spear field, the stone piles, and a black and white pony. Who needed playgrounds? And lucky me, the portal to this kid-size continent was the dead end of my new street named George.

I spent much of the next ten years in this houseless, streetless wilderness and in the park on the other side of the creek. Sometimes I was with others, sometimes alone. By the time the ten years were up, I had caught a handful of salamanders, hit a home run, raced against my stopwatch, searched for the Devil, kissed a girl, and bled from an attack of leeches.

But I did not go to sleep on the frontier side of the dead-end fence, or wake up there, or go to school there. And that was okay, because the civilized side also had something that seemed expressly made for me and my playmates, geographic features that appeared on no map, had no names, yet were intimately familiar to all kids in the neighborhood. Seen from above, they would appear as a second, nameless grid overlaid on the public one. I speak of alleyways.

To me and the neighborhood kids, the back of a house was more important than the front, and we happily roamed the alleyways that bordered our backyards. Alleys were sized to make us comfortable—with a running start, you could practically broad-jump across some of them. In an alley it was the car, not the kid, that was the intruder. Alleys were for sneakers and bikes and trikes and wagons.

Alleys had no rules, no signs. Danger and parental interference were minimal. You could lie on your back in the middle of an alley (if you wanted to) and close your eyes for five minutes and not be run over. You could hang the frame of an old wooden chair from a telephone pole spike and use it as a basketball rim. In an alley you could practice riding your new bike in peace, then ram it into potholes and get yourself thrown, like a bronco buster. You could check out other people's garbage cans. If you wanted.

If you ran away from home, or planned to, you would go by alleyway. The network of nameless alleys mimicked the town's official layout. You could go any-where—for all I knew, clear across the country.

With the frontier and the park and the alleys avail-able to us, you might think we would stay off the streets. We did not, of course. If it pleased us to get up a foot-ball game in the middle of the street or hide from seek-ers under parked cars, that's what we did. Because, in truth, our territory was wherever we happened to be. Whichever side of the dead end we were on, whichever side of the door, we confiscated the turf and made it our own.

And so, if we felt like resting, we would alight like a small flock of birds onto the nearest front steps. Except for those at the house directly across the street from

802. For reasons too vague for words, we were afraid of the man who lived there. His front steps were never sat on, his sidewalk never hopscotched, his doorbell never rung, his backyard fence never climbed. The truth was, he was simply a widowed barber who preferred to keep his shades down all the time, but try telling that to us.

Ten years, from six to sixteen. Ten years in the West End. Ten years of twin Popsicles and Bonomo's Turkish taffy, hightop Keds and a plaid cummerbund, Howdy Doody and Willie the Worm and Uncle Miltie on TV Tuesday nights, salamanders and snakes and candy cigarettes, coal dust on the clothesline, baseball cleats swinging from my handlebars, Ovaltine in my milk, knots in my yo-yo string.

War

I hate war. But when I was little, I loved it. War was a game, guns were toys, death an amusement ride. The first card game I ever played was called war.

I also played with little green soldiers, maybe two inches high. I loved their perfect, tiny helmets that reminded me of cereal bowls. Even the faces of the soldiers were perfect and green. Their tiny mouths and eyes were forever locked into a battlefield moment that I could only imagine.

I read G.I. Joe and Combat Kelly comic books. Then, down at the creek, I would poke a stick into the powdery bottom silt, pop it upward, and go "Boom!" I pretended the resulting brown underwater cloud was an atomic bomb explosion.

And of course, I played war with my friends. Beyond the dead end, there were two major arsenals: the stone piles and the spear field. The stone piles were on the other side of the tracks, between the main dump and the creek. There were five of them, each about ten feet high. The piles no doubt belonged to a construction company, but as far as we dead-end kids were concerned, they were there strictly in answer to our instinct to fling a stone.

Yet the one real stone battle I recall happened not there but at the creek (another inexhaustible source of stones; it wasn't called Stony Creek for nothing). We divided ourselves into two platoons and took up positions on either side of the creek. We loaded up and fired away.

The creek at that point was hardly wider than an alleyway. Across the water Johnny Seeton was firing from behind a tree. I waited till he poked his head out. He was looking right at me. I fired. I was aiming to hit him in the eyebrow. This is not as malicious as it sounds, for we were only playing at war—we were pretending, and everybody knew you didn't get hurt pretending. Besides, Johnny Seeton was one of my two best friends. And double-besides, who ever actually hit what they were aiming at?

The stone hit him in the eyebrow.

He screamed. He wouldn't stop screaming. Blood streamed down his face. He galloped across the water, ignoring stepping stones, screamed up the creek bank, and screamed all the way home. As for me, pretend did not give way to horror instantly. For several seconds of fanciful confusion, as Johnny Seeton thrashed wildly past me, I felt surprised that our relationship as best friends did not seem to count in this matter, as if a stone thrown by me should hurt him less.

Neither Johnny nor his parents ever said anything to me about the incident. They didn't have to. The two-week patch on Johnny's eye punished me every day.

Spears were safer.

Go to the dead end, turn left, walk up the tracks past Red Hill and the other, smaller dump, climb the trackside bluff, and you were in the spear field—so named for the plants growing there. Strip one of them of its leaves, and you were left with a sturdy four-foot-high stalk straight as a pool cue. Pluck it from the ground, shake off the root dirt, and bring on the enemy.

As I passed through the grade-school years, war became less about machine-gun chatter and spectacular explosions and more about people.

I read about war, about the bodies of soldiers, even enemy soldiers, whose lifeless hands clutched photographs of loved ones back home.

I read of the torture of captive troops. I especially cringed over the fingernail torture, in which a pair of pliers pulled out the victim's fingernails, slowly, one by one. Such things happened to spies and to people who knew too many secrets. I resolved that if I was ever in a war, I would be a dumb nonspy.

But I could not resolve not to be a soldier. Every passing day, every February 1—the date of my birth—prodded me closer to the ominous cloud that hung over my future. It was called the draft, and it meant that when I (and all other boys deemed healthy enough) got out of high school or college, I would have to join the armed forces whether I wanted to or not.

As if to prepare me, my daydreams placed me in grim

wartime situations. I saw myself, apparently a failure at avoiding secrets, in the hands of enemy interrogators.

"Tell us," they growl.

"Never," I say firmly, for I am a good American soldier.

Then I feel the pliers grip the end of the nail on my right index finger, and cold sweat pours from me, and I feel the tug of the pliers and then the pain begins—and I sing. I sing like the Vienna Boys' Choir. I empty my head like a box of cornflakes. I tell them everything from our deepest military secrets to my shoe size.

And I anguish. Because, though I realize this is only a daydream, I am afraid that if such a thing ever really happens, I will play my part poorly. I am afraid that I will crack during torture. I am ashamed that I cannot measure up to a captive spy I once read about, whose lips were still sealed after losing all ten fingernails.

Sometimes in my fearful fantasies my captors bypassed torture and simply marched me out to the firing squad. But I never got shot. Even as six rifle sights met at my trembling heart—"Ready! Aim!"—I call out to the commanding officer, "Wait a minute!"

The commanding officer pauses.

"There's something you don't know. If you shoot me you'll never find out."

The officer calls off the guns. He expects me to divulge vital military secrets, but the information I offer is purely personal. I tell him something about his wife, his family back home, something he could never have known without me. He is overcome with gratitude. He dismisses the firing squad. And I have discovered something: Words can save me.

Despite all the attention I paid to warfare, I was never in a real fight. Around sixth grade this began to bother me. I saw other kids flailing and clubbing, tearing each other's shirts to shreds, trading bloody noses, and I said to myself, "Hey, why not me?" I began to feel deprived because my right hand had never known the feel of fist on chin. I felt a growing need to hit somebody.

But who? I could think of no one I wanted to hit. And apparently nobody wanted to hit me. Every day I walked to and from school unchallenged. I was a bur in no one's saddle. A likable bloke.

However, the prospect of going through life punchless was too strong to ignore. I looked around my classroom. Who was as small as I, or better yet, even smaller? Who was unlikely to hit me back? Who needed hitting?

There was only one answer: Joey Stackhouse.

Joey Stackhouse was skinny. Mash down his blond pompadour and he was maybe half an inch shorter than I. He had a narrow, foxy face. But his main feature was teeth. He was a walking warning against not brushing. When he smiled, you found yourself looking at all the colors in your crayon box. Plus his clothes were shabby.

For several days I hung close to Joey, alert for an offending remark or gesture. He remained obstinately harmless, as friendly as ever. It became clear that I myself would have to manufacture the momentum for the punch.

I worked myself into a snit. I convinced myself that anybody with teeth like that was asking for it. One day he walked home with me after school. We were on the 700 block of George Street, close to my house. I picked a fight with him, accused him of something, I don't remember what. Then I hit him. I balled my fist and swung, and when my knuckles landed—*thock*—against his chin bone, I was as surprised as when my stone hit Johnny Seeton.

As punches go, it was dainty, more tap than wallop, my intention being to match a punch's form, not force. I'm sure that, physically, he barely felt it. But a punch has a double impact, as I was about to learn, and only the first lands on the chin. Joey's eyes widened. He stood there staring at me with such wild astonishment that I knew at once he had not, not in a million years, been asking for it. He started to cry. He blurted out, "Why'd you do that?" and ran back down George Street.

If ever I had notions of becoming a warrior, they died that day as I turned the other way and walked home alone. It has been more than forty years since I hit Joey Stackhouse—the first and last person I ever punched— and it remains the only taste of war I ever needed.

Lash La Rue

Early on I learned, without anyone actually telling me, that in this world it is not enough just to *be*. You have to *be something*.

So around the age of five I decided to be a cowboy.

Cowboys rode three trails into my life: (1) The Garrick Movie Theater downtown, which showed Western double features on Saturday afternoons, (2) comic books, and (3) *Frontier Playhouse*.

Frontier Playhouse came on TV every weeknight at six, right after *Howdy Doody* and right in the middle of dinnertime. I was not allowed to eat in the living room, where the TV was, but I was allowed to move my chair to the doorway between the kitchen and dining room. I placed my dinner on the seat, knelt down, and watched the nightly cowboy movie while eating on my knees. It's a wonder I could see the platter-size screen at the far end of the house.

From TV and movies and comics I knew lots of cowboys: Roy Rogers, Gene Autry, Hopalong Cassidy, Lash La Rue, Red Ryder, Tom Mix, the Lone Ranger, Tex Ritter, Ranger Joe, Tim McCoy, Hoot Gibson. And horses: Trigger, Topper, Silver, Champion, Tony, Buttermilk.

When my friends and I played cowboys, almost everyone wanted to be Roy Rogers. With his fringed shirts and silky neckerchief and white hat and golden horse, how could you not want to be Roy? I was usually the first to call out, "I'll be Roy Rogers!"

But when I was alone and my secrets came peeping out from their hiding places, I knew there was a cowboy I wanted to be even more than Roy Rogers. I wanted to be Lash La Rue. From hat to boots, Lash La Rue dressed all in black. But that wasn't what made Lash La Rue special—it was the whip. He carried it coiled at his belt, and with it he did most everything the others did with their six-shooters. Was a bad guy reaching for his gun? Lash was quicker with his whip. A flick of the wrist, the whip uncoils—leather lightning!—darts ten, twenty, thirty feet across the dust to snatch the gun, barely clear of its holster, from the bad guy's hand. Is the bad guy running away? The whip catches him at the ankles, trips and hogties him, ready for the sheriff. The rawhide tongue could lick the spit from a horse's lips or kiss it on the ear.

Lash La Rue. I recognized him as "cool" before I ever knew the word.

I loved the West. The songs: "Home on the Range," "Tumbling Tumbleweeds," "Red River Valley." Cattle drives. Sarsaparilla. (The movies made sarsaparilla seem like liquid fire. Imagine my surprise, years later, when I drank my first glass—and discovered it was root beer.)

Stagecoach holdups. Box canyons. Harmonicas and campfires and coyotes howling in the night.

I had an armament Roy Rogers himself would have been proud to own: twin golden pistols in twin white leather holsters. My white leather gun belt had a dozen little leather loops to hold a dozen red wooden bullets. Of course, the bullets were just for show. The real ammo was caps, five rolls to a box. They could be bought at one of two grocery stores, Freilich's next door or Teufel's across the street.

I drew pictures of good guys and bad guys shooting it out. I considered myself an expert at drawing horses, but my favorite part I always saved for last: the orange, red, and yellow streaks that indicated gunfire crisscrossing the picture.

My early cowboy artwork.

I practiced my draw until it was as fast as Tim McCoy's. I twirled my golden guns on my fingers. I drank my Ovaltine from a Ranger Joe mug. I played the harmonica. I yodeled.

And then one day in third grade I went all the way. When I woke up, instead of getting dressed as usual, I put on my cowboy outfit: ten-gallon hat, studded shirt, jodhpurs, golden guns, boots and spurs. My mother must have thought, *Oh, no!* as she heard my spurs clanking toward the breakfast table. I drew plenty of stares on my three-block walk to school.

Such was the class facing our teacher, Miss Davis, that morning: twenty-five pupils and one cowboy. She probably checked her calendar to see if this was Halloween. I remember her looking down at me in the first row, smiling gently, and saying, "Jerry, would you like to do something for us?" Apparently I did, for I stood, faced the class, and serenaded them with "I Got Spurs That Jingle Jangle Jingle." And I shook my boots.

A couple of summers later I had a chance to really live the cowboy life. I had gotten a pup tent for Christmas. Now I could camp out, pretend I was on a cattle drive, pretend our backyard was a tumbleweed range somewhere in Texas or Wyoming.

I invited my other best friend, Roger Adelman, to join me. We laid out our blankets in the tent. We talked and played card games, and as the sun went down we turned on a battery-powered lantern and played some more. Eventually it was time to go to bed. We crawled under our covers and turned off the lantern.

An hour later I was still awake. I had never known it got so dark on the range. And so quiet. No cows mooing, no coyotes calling, only Roger's breathing. And the ground—even with a blanket it was so hard. How did cattle stand it? In vain I kept trying to sleep. I felt immense and bristling, the only soul awake on the planet. I longed for a night-light.

When I couldn't stand it any longer, I shook Roger awake. Five minutes later he was trudging homeward while I climbed into my bed, in my bedroom. Alas, I was not at home on the range after all. I was strictly a living-room cowboy.

Ashes in the Grass

Two years after wearing my cowboy getup to school, I donned an outfit of a different sort. It was a Saturday morning in September, and I was getting ready for my first organized athletic event: a grade-school football league game. First I pulled shoulder pads over my undershirt; then I put on my number 15 blue and white football shirt; then my football pants with knee pads; then my sneakers; then my football helmet. Looking in the mirror, I could hardly find myself in all that armor.

I was a nervous fifth grader. Most of the players would be sixth graders, so I did not protest when my mother offered to go with me. We walked down George to the dead end and along the dirt path to the park. The field was swarming with kids from the six public grade schools in town, and none of them looked like me. No helmets, no shoulder pads—just T-shirts and jeans (which we called dungarees). The only thing we had in common was sneakers.

What had I expected? I had known this was two-hand touch football.

I was mortified. I dared not approach my team, Hartranft Elementary. My mother and I stood at a distance, watching the game in awkward silence. I prayed no one would recognize me.

Officially, then, my athletic career began a week later, when I arrived dressed like everybody else, and without a mother in tow.

My cowboy boots, spurs still attached, grew dusty on the floor of my bedroom closet. The twin white holsters and golden guns hung over one of the maple posts at the foot of my bed. As the years went by, the red toy bullets disappeared one by one, until only empty ammo loops were left.

I had given up cowboys for quarterbacks, horses for stitched horsehide. No longer were my seasons summer, fall, winter, and spring but baseball, football, and basketball. I was a sports nut.

Sports had taken their hold on me, even at age 6. I'm getting the autograph of Gil Dodds, a mile-run champion (and minister).

Perhaps it was inevitable. Not long after I belted my last ball over the landlady's fence on Marshall Street, my father had begun taking me to Norristown High School games, basketball at first, then football and track and field. He was a ticket collector for football games, scorekeeper for basketball, and would hold those jobs for over fifty years. The world of sports had simply been waiting for me to grow into it.

We took our sports seriously, my friends and I, getting up games to fill every spare moment. Lunchtime at school, for example. We had an hour and a half, as I recall, since Hartranft had no cafeteria and all students went home to eat. I ran the three blocks to my house, wolfed down my lunch, and ran back, leaving me with an hour and fifteen minutes to play basketball on the playground. It's a won-der the teacher didn't pass out deodorant when afternoon lessons began.

We played wherever we could: alleys, streets, play-grounds, the park, even living rooms. But there was one special place. My old friend Roger Adelman, in a letter to me, describes it perfectly:

"This field was unique. We played baseball there, but it really wasn't set up for baseball. There wasn't a right field, since what would have been right field was occupied by the stand of spear weeds which, for some mystic reason, no one would (or could) cut down (although it was burned down several times by Bill Zollers, the neighborhood fire-bug). So all players had to bat right-handed—or promise not to pull the ball to right field. The outfield—left and center—was full of weeds and rough spots but was playable. The infield was in good shape because Johnny Rizzuto and I mowed the grass regularly. We also marked the foul lines with white ashes from the coal-burning furnaces in our houses.

"Left field was a special place. The boundary of deep left field was the dump. If you hit one into the dump in the air, you got a home run. If the ball took one bounce into the dump, you got a double. If it rolled in, you got a single. Only qualified players were assigned to left field: fast enough to stop those bouncers and rollers from going into the dump, brave enough to run right up to the edge of the dump and snag a liner headed into it (I have a memory of Pickles Noblett taking a header into the dump after a valiant try to stop a home run), and daring enough to go down into the dump to dig out a ball that ended up there. The dump had its own mystique—not to mention rats—and I am sure that, to this day, there are still a few hardballs there."

I envied my playmates their nicknames. Besides Pickles Noblett, there were Boogie Batson, Yock Doyle, Booper O'Hara, and Buffalo Morris. My own nickname was Spit—their choice, not mine.

For my money, the best player of all was Jerry Fox. He was several years older than I, and a dead-end legend. He was not very fast, but he did not have to be, for he was magically elusive. This talent came most prominently into play in street football. Sometimes he would just stand there, the ball cradled in his arm, one foot on the bumper of a parked car, daring us to tag him. We reached for his arm—it was gone; for his stomach—gone. Each body part was under separate control, free to move in all directions. It was like trying to tag an eel. If Jerry Fox were a letter of the alphabet, he would have been an S. He was untouchable. His nickname said it all: "The Pro."

Summers gave us time to gorge on sports. On a typical summer day I dropped my baseball glove into the chrome-plated basket of my bicycle and pedaled out the dirt path to the Little League field at the park. Other guys came from other directions. The rest of the day went like this: Play baseball until lunch, pedal home to eat, pedal back to the park (this time with basketball in bike basket), play basketball at park court until dinner, pedal home to eat, return for more basketball until dark.

Next day: Do it again.

I'm in the back row (with a cap), a finalist in a foul-shooting contest in the park (age 12, 1953). On my right is Dennis Magee, whose last name I gave to a character called Maniac.

Never the Monkey

In a green metal box in a bedroom closet, tucked into a fuzzy gray cotton pouch, lies the most cherished memento of my grade-school days. It is a gold-plated medal no bigger than a postage stamp. Inscribed on the back are the words "50-YARD DASH—CHAMPION."

The medal came from the only official race I ever participated in. There were many unofficial ones...

"Race you to the store!"

"Last one in's a monkey!"

"Ready...Set...Go!"

Like kids the world over, we raced to determine the fastest. In the early 1950s on the 800 block of George Street in the West End of Norristown, Pennsylvania, that was me. I was usually the winner, and never the monkey.

I reached my peak at the age of twelve. That summer I led the Norristown Little League in stolen bases. In an all-star playoff game I did something practically unheard of: I was safe at first base on a ground ball to the pitcher.

Some days I pulled my sneaker laces extra tight and went down to the railroad tracks. The cinders there had the feel of a running track. I measured off fifty or a hundred yards and sprinted the distance, timing myself with my father's stopwatch. Sometimes, heading back to the starting line, I tried to see how fast I could run on the railroad ties. Sometimes I ran on the rail.

It was during that year that I won my medal. I represented Hartranft in the fifty-yard dash at the annual track-and-field meet for the Norristown grade schools. The meet was held at Roosevelt Field, where the high school track and football teams played.

Favored to win the race was Laverne Dixon of Gotwals Elementary. "Froggy," as he was known to everyone but his teachers, had won the fifty-yard dash the year before as a mere fifth grader. Surely he would win again. My goal was to place second.

When the starter barked, "Ready!" I got into position: one knee and ten fingertips on the cinder track. I knew what to do from the many meets I had attended with my father. I glanced to my left and right and saw nothing but shins—everyone else was standing. I could not have known it then, but the race was already mine.

I was off with the gun. My memory of those fifty yards has nothing to do with sprinting but rather with two sensations. The first was surprise that I could not see any other runners. This led to a startling conclusion: *I must be ahead!* Which led to the second sensation: an anxious expectation, a waiting to be overtaken.

I never was. I won.

Froggy Dixon didn't even come in second. That went to Billy Steinberg, a stranger then, who would become my best friend in junior high school. He would also grow to be faster than I, as would many of my schoolmates. But that was yet to come. For the moment, as I slowed down and trotted into a sun the color and dazzle of the medal I was about to receive, I knew only the wonder of seven astounding seconds when no one was ahead of me.

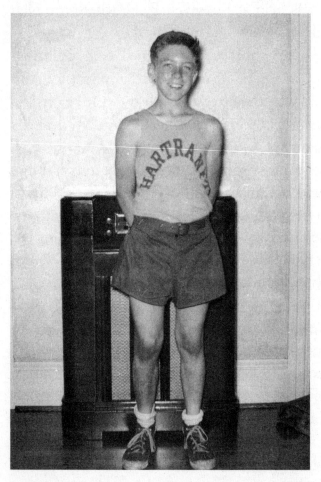

The fifty-yard-dash champion for Hartranft Elementary (age 12, 1953).

Shortstop

From ages eleven to sixteen, if someone asked me what I wanted to be when I grew up, I gave one of two answers: "A baseball player" or "A shortstop."

Major league baseball—that was the life for me. And I wanted to live it only as a shortstop. When I trotted onto a diamond, I instinctively headed for the dusty plain between second and third. I never wanted to play any other position. When we got up sandlot games, no one else occupied shortstop. They knew it was mine.

I was eleven when I first played Little League baseball. To give as many kids as possible a chance to participate, the Little League declared that some of us would share uniforms with others. And so the season was exactly half over when I pedaled my bike up to Albert Pascavage's house to pick up his uniform: green socks, green cap, gray woolen shirt, and pants with green trim. I packed my precious cargo into my bike basket and drove it carefully home. I was a member of the Green Sox.

During one game in that half season I played second base—apparently no one told the manager I was going to be a major league shortstop. Our opponent was the Red Sox. The batter hit a ground ball right at me. I crouched, feet spread, glove ready, as I had been taught in the *Times Herald* baseball school. I could hear the ball crunching along the sandy ground. It hit my glove—but not the pocket. Instead it glanced off the fat leather thumb and rolled on behind me.

Shortshop, Green Sox
(age 12, 1953).

My first error!

I was heartbroken. I stomped my foot. I pounded my fist into the stupid glove.

When the inning was over and I slunk to the Green Sox bench, the manager was waiting for me. I thought he was going to console me. I thought he would say, "Tough luck, Jerry. Nice try," and then tousle my hair.

That's not what happened.

What he really did was glare angrily at me, and what he really said was, "Don't you ever do that again." He pointed out that while I was standing there pounding my glove, two Red Sox runs had scored. "Next time you miss the ball, you turn around and chase it down. You don't just stand there feeling sorry for yourself. Understand?"

I nodded. And I never forgot.

Like most of the kids in my class, I got better at sports simply by growing older. I went from being one of the worst players in Little League as an eleven-year-old to making the all-star team as a twelve-year-old. The following year I was the only seventh grader to start on the Stewart Junior High School team—at shortstop, of course. It mattered little that I was not very good at hitting a curve ball, since most pitchers threw only fastballs.

During the summer of junior high school I played in a baseball league called Connie Mack Knee-Hi, for thirteen- to fifteen-year-olds. Before each game, one team would line up along the first-base line, the other team along third base. The umpire stood on the pitcher's mound, took off his cap, and read aloud the Sportsmanship Pledge, pausing after each line so the rest of us could repeat it in chorus. We pledged ourselves to be loyal to, among other things, "clean living and clean speech." In the final line we promised to be "a generous victor and a gracious loser."

In the Knee-Hi summer of 1955, I had little chance to be a gracious loser. My team, Norristown Brick Company, swept through the local league undefeated, winning our games by an average score of 12–1. One score was 24–0. One team simply refused to show up. Our pitchers threw four no-hitters, three by Lee Holmes. Opposing batters could no more hit Bill Bryzgornia's fastball than spell his name. We were a powerhouse.

We beat Conshohocken two out of three to gain the state playoffs. Three wins there put us into the title game. On a bright Saturday afternoon at War Memorial Field in Doylestown, Norristown Brick Company defeated Ellwood City, 4–2, to become Connie Mack Knee-Hi champions of Pennsylvania.

In the awards ceremony after the game, we were given jackets saying STATE CHAMPIONS. Ellwood City players got trophies. A jacket would eventually wear out and be thrown away, leaving me with nothing to show for our great triumph. But a trophy was immune to frayed cuffs and moth holes. A trophy would be forever. I watched as each Ellwood City player walked up for his trophy and half-wished I had been on the losing side.

A week later, during a banquet at the Valley Forge Hotel in downtown Norristown, to my relief, we were each given a magnificent trophy.

Two buddies (Anthony Greco and Bob Hopple) and me (left), heading off to dance at Grace Lutheran Church, 1955. I'm wearing my Knee-Hi State Champions jacket.

Chucking dust on a four-base diamond was only part of the baseball life. There was the long list of major league batting averages to pore over each Sunday in *The Philadelphia Inquirer*. There was the baseball encyclopedia, my first history book, to study. Long before I knew the difference between Yorktown and Gettysburg, I knew Ty Cobb's lifetime batting average (.367) and Cy Young's total career pitching victories (511).

There were cards to flip. We bought Fleer's bubblegum just to get the baseball cards, and then we dueled. Slip one corner of the card between forefinger and middle finger and flip outward, Frisbee-like, toward a wall. The kid whose card lands closest to the wall picks up the other kid's card. The stacks of cards I won this way would be worth a fortune today if I had kept them.

There were baseballs to tape. Seldom in our sandlot games did we have a ball with a real stitched horsehide cover still on it. Most often the balls were covered in black utility tape. A white ball was a real treat. It meant that someone had sneaked into the medicine chest at home and used up half a roll of first-aid tape.

There were hours to spend bouncing tennis balls off neighbors' brick walls, any wall but that of the mysterious barber across the street. For hours each week I scooped up the rebounding grounders, practicing to be a great shortstop. Considering the thumping I gave those houses, it's a wonder I was never chased off. Maybe the people behind the walls understood that in my mind I was not really standing on George Street but in the brown dust of Connie Mack Stadium, out at shortstop, fielding hot shots off the bat of Willie Mays.

And there was the glove. My glove bore the signature of Marty Marion, slick-fielding shortstop of the St. Louis Cardinals.

Each year at the end of summer vacation, I rubbed my glove with olive oil from the kitchen cabinet. Then I pressed a baseball deep into the pocket of the glove, curled the leather fingers about the ball, and squeezed the whole thing into a shoebox. Standing on a chair, I set the box high on a closet shelf. Baseball season was officially over.

For the next six months we would hibernate, shortstop and glove, dreaming of the Chiclets-white bases at Connie Mack Stadium, feeling in the palm the hard, round punch of a grounder well caught.

Good Boy

Like cowboys and then sports, grade school was a constant presence in my life, though not an especially interesting one. It seems to me that most interesting stories about grade school are told by kids who got in trouble. I never got in trouble. I was, as they say, a Good Boy.

But what is a Good Boy? From the world's point of view, it is a boy who appears to be good. The key word here is *appears*. For I believe that beneath the appearance of most Good Boys is a Bad Boy waiting to break out. Oh, I don't mean bad in the sense of committing crimes or hurting people. I mean bad in the sense of, say, leaving a wad of chewing gum on the teacher's chair. Or washing the blackboard with spit. Or jumping up from your seat in the middle of silent reading, standing on top of your desk, raising your fists to the ceiling, and roaring with all your might, "Phooey!"

That kind of bad.

Let me tell you something about the Good Boy: Just because he doesn't get into trouble doesn't mean he doesn't appreciate trouble. I know I did. I understood what a boring world this would be without the troublemakers. And so I was a big fan of Leonard Wilfong, who was always getting into trouble. I didn't exactly stand up and applaud when Leonard did something bad, but I gave him my undivided attention, and if I thought I could get away with it, I laughed.

To the Bad Boy, that's the reward: laughter. It's the payoff of a deal that is never spoken of, never written down, yet is understood perfectly by the kids in class. It's as if back on the first day of first grade, all the boys had a secret meeting and one of them was voted to be Bad Boy. He—in our case, Leonard Wilfong—accepted the job, along with the punishments that would surely fall to him, with the understanding that the rest of us would (1) pay attention and (2) laugh.

And the meeting broke up and Leonard Wilfong went forth and did outrageous things, and we laughed. Neither Leonard nor the rest of us understood this, but in a sense we were laughing at ourselves, for Leonard Wilfong was the embodiment of the Bad Boy in all of us. Leonard did what we did not have the nerve to do. Leonard did not have the same fears we had. He feared spelling tests and long division and report cards. He did not fear trouble. He did not fear rules. And though we did not envy Leonard Wilfong his punishments or his bad grades, we absolutely envied him his recklessness. We respected him as the representative of that which was secret in ourselves. We saluted him with our attention and our laughter.

When the teacher wasn't looking.

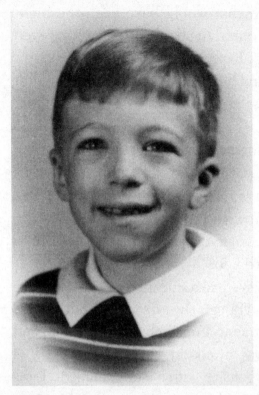

At age 6 (1947):
a Good Boy in the making.

So if you want an interesting Hartranft Elementary School autobiography from those days, go see Leonard Wilfong. As for me, I have already mentioned the fifty-yard dash and my spur-song serenade. Only four other interesting things happened to me in grade school:

1. Second grade. This did not happen directly to me but to a calf. Mrs. Care, our teacher, lived on a farm. One spring day she took the whole class there for a visit. While jumping into the hay in the barn, Roger Adelman landed on a pitchfork and had to go to the

hospital. Ordinarily, that would have been the high-light of the day, but out in the barnyard something even more interesting was happening.

A mother cow and her calf were hanging around just inside the fence, close enough for some of us to reach out and touch. Then, as we watched in amazement, the mother—who, you must understand, was a lot taller than her offspring—backed up to the calf and pooped on its head. Until Mrs. Care finally wiped it off, the plop just stayed there, like a brown beret. Was it my imagination, or did the calf really have an expression on its face, as if to say, "Hey, Ma—wha'd I do?"

2. Second grade. We had a student teacher from West Chester University. Though she was careful not to give me preferential treatment, I remember feeling proud and special. Why? She was my cousin, Dolly.

3. Third grade. I got sick with a kidney ailment. I was in the hospital for ten days and out of school for two months. My mother tells me that in the hospital I put on a brave front. She says that whenever she and my father visited me, I chatted away happily with them. Then, the second they left the room, I started to cry. My mother found this out from the nurses. Personally, I don't remember. My mother also says they gave me so many needles in the hospital that my rear end looked like a pincushion. I don't remember that either. As a reward for all the needles each night, a smiling nurse in a candy-striped uniform brought me a milkshake. That I remember.

4. Sixth grade. In early spring of that year the two sixth grades were brought together for a series of spelling bees. Since I won more of them than anyone else, I was declared spelling champion of Hartranft Elementary. That honor earned me the chance to compete in the Montgomery County spelling bee, the winner of which would go to Washington, D.C., for the national bee.

As a sixth grader among contestants ranging up to eighth grade, I was one of the youngest on the stage at Norristown High School that night in April 1953. I don't think it ever occurred to me to try to win. My goal was to survive until at least the fourth round, since I had been told that no one from Hartranft had ever gotten that far.

Ninety-six school champions sat in long curved rows of folding chairs. Hanging on a string from everyone's neck was a square of white cardboard with a large black number. Mine was thirteen. Before the competition began, the master of ceremonies announced to the auditorium that we were honored to have last year's county champion with us—Nancy Ann Hammerschmidt of North Wales. He then turned from the audience to the stage and asked Nancy Ann to stand and take a bow, and who should stand up but number twelve, the pretty blond older girl sitting next to me.

The competition got under way. The opening words were easy, and most of us made it through the first two rounds. Then we started dropping like flies. When somebody misspelled a word—*bong!*—the judge hammered a big brassy bell and the kid was gone. No arguing, no whining—wham, bam, next, please.

Meanwhile back in the seats Nancy Ann Hammerschmidt and I were chatting away. Actually, Nancy Ann did most of the chatting. I mostly nodded and smiled in wonder that the famous, glamorous fourteen-year-old champion would be so familiar with the likes of me. When we returned to our seats after nailing our third-round words, Nancy Ann took out her wallet and showed me a picture of her boyfriend.

When in the fourth round Nancy Ann spelled "ecstasy" with a second *c* instead of an *s*, I was sure no bong would dare banish her from the stage. But it did, and off she marched. And so did I a few seconds later, having spelled lacquer "l-a-c-q-u-o-r." Considering how smitten I was with Nancy Ann, I'm surprised I even bothered to take my last turn at the mike before following her off the stage. She must have made a quick exit, though, for she was not among the growing crowd of misspellers behind the curtain, nor did I ever see her again. I guess neither Nancy Ann Hammerschmidt nor the spelling bee bonger cared that I was a Good Boy.

George
Street

Baseball is still baseball, and school is school, but George Street is no more. Oh, sure, if you travel to Norristown today and go west on Elm, you'll come to a street sign that says GEORGE. Don't believe it.

A street sign does not make a street. A time makes a street, and a people of that time. The sign will tell you nothing, nor will the people who live there today. Go ahead, ask them. Ask them whose front steps they better not sit on. Challenge them to a game of chew-the-peg. (Flip penknife from shoulder. If it doesn't stick in ground, pull out planted peg with teeth.) Or just stand there on the sidewalk outside 802 and close your eyes and listen for the avalanche of coal. Listen for days. You won't hear it. George Street is as gone as 1950.

I heard it. I heard it on coal day. Nearly every house on the block had a coal-burning furnace. In a front corner of the cellar, beneath the living room, was a plank-walled bin. It held a ton of coal. When the coal truck came, my job was to run to the cellar and open the window above the bin. The truck turned sideways in the street and backed up to the curb. From under the truck bed the coal man pulled the chute, which looked like a sliding board, and fed it through the open cellar window and into our bin. He lifted the hatch and the coal started coming, avalanching down the chute with such a racket that I had to clamp my hands over my ears. I had to tie a hanky around my nose, too, because of the coal dust that made a black, choking blizzard. I would crouch down under the washtub, fold my arms about my head, and wait out the bombardment from the enemy battleship and its sixteen-inch guns. Or if I wasn't pretending that day, I simply ran outside.

Softer sounds came from the Victrola. The Victrola was an early phonograph, a record player. Ours was portable, like a small boxy suitcase. Whenever I lifted the hinged cover I was treated to a special scent, a sweet dustiness that suggested slumbering songs, music's bunkhouse. To get the thing to work I had to crank it, like an old Model T Ford. The crank was a stepped metal rod with a black wooden egg-shaped handle. I placed a record on the turntable, then inserted the rod into a hole in the side of the player and cranked away. I flipped a switch, and the record began to spin. Breathlessly I lowered the needle to the smooth black edge of the disc. The needle slipped into the first groove, and "Too-ra-loo-ra-loo-ral"…Bing Crosby was crooning.

The main sound machine, of course, was the radio. Unlike many people my age, I cannot give a long list of the programs I listened to. What I do recall are three motifs: the Lone Ranger theme song, otherwise known as the *William Tell* Overture, footsteps walking down hallways, and doors creaking open. Beyond that I simply remember listening. And picturing.

For radio was a partnership. The radio furnished the sounds, and the listener supplied the pictures. TV and movie screens have shaded us from the evocative power of sound. Our eyes enslave us. "Seeing is believing." In contrast to TV, which asks us merely to turn it on and become a passive dartboard, radio asked us to meet it halfway, to co-create the moment. The resulting pictures in our heads had a depth of reality possible only when the camera is the person.

Despite my love of radio, I soon gave in to the lure of television.

The first TV set in my corner of the West End belonged to the Beswicks up on Kohn Street, a block west of George. Butchie Beswick's popularity zoomed. Day after day a mob of kids sat on the Beswick living room rug after school, goggle-eyed and gaping like so many guppies at *Willie the Worm* on the ten-inch black and white screen. Mrs. Beswick must have been a saint. Over time the mob diminished, one cross-legged floor-sitter at a time, as new families acquired television sets.

Our family got one in 1950—a twelve-inch Magnavox—when I was in third grade and home with my kidney illness. Doctor's orders confined me to my bed, but I made such a fuss that I was finally allowed to be carried downstairs and plopped in a chair to watch TV for one hour, not a minute more.

Television and I grew up together; meanwhile movies seduced me with Technicolor and 3-D and CinemaScope. By the time I got my driver's license, the only radio in my life was in the family car.

On July 20, 1969, *Apollo 11* astronauts rode the lunar module *Eagle* to the surface of the moon. Like much of the world, I was in front of a TV set watching fuzzy images of the event: *Eagle* launching from the mother spacecraft, *Eagle* orbiting the moon, *Eagle* coming in lower, lower, skimming lunar hills and craters, seeking a spot to land. I strained my eyes watching, and still I wasn't seeing, not well enough...*the pictures in my head.* I rushed outside to my car, I turned on the radio, and that's where I experienced the landing on the moon. I had rediscovered what I knew back on George Street: *listening* is believing.

And so is remembering, remembering George Street:

Cooling myself with a Popsicle stick fan...playing chew-the-peg..."smoking" punk...digging up the grass between the front-walk bricks (my most hated chore after taking out the garbage)...Mr. Freilich's long-handled grocery grippers, allowing him to reach to the highest shelf and pull down a box of cereal...purple ribbons on a door, meaning someone had died in that house...pouring Morton salt on the fat summer slugs that left silver trails across the bricks...Quaker Oats...bathtub-shaped Hudson cars...the bug truck spraying everything, including me, with mosquito poison...cat's-eye marbles in the dirt...Bono's fruit and vegetable bus...on a winter morning, a slow white plug of cream pushing up the cap of the milk bottle on our front step...the bread man...the rag man...the rag man's horse, itself slow and drooping as a sack of rags, as if every *clop* upon the street would be its last...the rag man's mournful warbling bleat: "Raaaaaaags!"...the sad, slow syncopation passing George, heading for Kohn, Noble, Buttonwood, westward..."Raaaaaaags!" *clop-clop*, "Raaaaaags!" *clop-clop*....

Mrs. Seeton's
Whistle

More than a Victrola crank handle or the blizzard of coal dust, George Street was its people. It is something I understand better now than I did then. I can find old marbles and baseball cards in antique shops and rummage sales. I wish I could find the people there, too. I have so much to ask them.

I have questions for the Freilich family, who operated the grocery store next to us, on the corner of George and Elm. The Freilichs were, I believe, the only Jews on the block, and to live next to them was on some days like living next to another country.

Nothing but a thin wire fence separated our backyards. On most days the Freilichs' backyard was just like ours: trash barrel and garbage can, a flower bed or two, a clothesline, a walkway down the middle to the back gate. But on certain Sundays in summer there suddenly appeared in the Freilichs' backyard people such as I had never seen. The men especially were distinctive, for they dressed all in black and wore black hats and long shaggy beards. Afraid to stare openly at them, I ran upstairs to my bedroom window and stared until my eyeballs ached.

Next day on the way to school I usually saw Nancy Freilich. Nancy was the older of two sisters. She was thin and had long red hair and walked pigeon-toed in her black and white saddle shoes. She was very bright and friendly, and she would have made a terrific friend, but she was a year older and a grade ahead of me, and fifth-grade boys did not mix much with sixth-grade girls, even if they were next-door neighbors. So I did not ask Nancy Freilich about the black-suited shaggy-bearded people in her backyard the day before. And instead of becoming terrific friends, we simply smiled and waved and said hi to each other.

Nancy's older brother Morton was seldom seen on George Street. Unlike most of us, who seemed to have sprouted like grass from the cracks between the side-walk bricks, Morton Freilich occupied a higher plane. He was brilliant. He became a doctor. He made people well. But he could not make himself well. Morton had always had a bad case of asthma. Sometimes it was hard for him to breathe.

So he moved himself and his medical practice to Arizona. I pictured him arriving in that faraway state, smiling to see the palm trees and desert sands and adobe-style houses. I pictured him looking up at the cloudless sky and throwing out his arms and going "Ahhh!" and for the first time in his life taking a long, deep clean breath of air. And maybe he did, but within several years the asthma had tracked him down and killed him, Morton Freilich in Arizona, only in his thirties, brilliant, the grocer's son.

Nancy's little sister was Sharon. From the day she was born, some kids on the street, I don't remember who, seemed to have it in for her. They were always saying unkind things about her. I remember thinking, Why? What did she do? I could understand people getting mad at someone who was always bugging them, but Sharon Freilich had just been *born*. She hadn't had time to bug anyone. I wondered if there was a secret that I had missed.

I began to study little Sharon Freilich as she toddled about the grocery store and the brick sidewalk outside. I tried to detect what it was in her that offended others. I saw her sitting one day on the front step of the store. Her knees were smudged, and I thought, Is *that* it? Dirty knees?

She wasn't just sitting there, she was crying. I looked around to see if someone had said something mean to her, but the block was deserted, and I did not understand that an ugly word, once spoken, once heard, remains in the ear forever. Seeing her cry, alone and dirty-kneed on the front step, as alone as I've ever seen anybody in my life, I tried not to feel bad, because I knew so many others who would not have felt bad, who would have laughed. But I failed.

On the other side of us, at 804, lived the Corys. Virginia, the younger of two sisters, was a year behind me in school. We played together at first, then less and less as we got older.

My enduring memory of Virginia Cory centers on a particular Fourth of July at Elmwood Park. She was about fourteen years old and had entered herself in the annual talent show at the band shell. When she was announced, she walked onstage and sang a romantic ballad called "Too Young":

> "They try to tell us we're too young
> Too young to really be in love..."

Her normally pale cheeks were red as apples as she sang earnestly—and off-key—into the microphone:

> "They say that love's a word,
> A word we've only heard
> And can't begin to know the meaning of..."

Out in the audience I felt uncomfortable, even embarrassed. I wondered if the people sitting around me knew that Virginia Cory was my next-door neighbor. Didn't she know she was off-key? What ever made her think she could win a talent contest? Why doesn't she stop? I wondered. But she went on singing and singing into the microphone until the very last note:

> "And then someday they may recall
> We were not too young at all."

She took a bow and left the stage. People politely clapped. Naturally she did not win, not even the lowest of honorable mentions. But that was it. What had registered as a catastrophe with me left the rest of the world unfazed. They did not cancel the pet show or the fireworks that night, and Virginia herself, to my knowledge, did not spend a single minute under her bed hiding in shame.

If I met her today, I would like to tell her that when I think of my favorite songs of those days, I think of Les Paul and Mary Ford singing "Tennessee Waltz" and the Chordettes singing "Mr. Sandman" and Virginia Cory singing "Too Young." I would tell her that I play it often in the jukebox of my memory. I would ask her to sing it again, and this time to honor her moxie, I would clap long and loud.

Spider Sukoloski lived next to the Corys, at 806. Spider's given name was Eugene, but no one (except maybe his mother) called him that. Spider's hair was long and dark blond and combed back and cemented with Brylcreem. Spider wore his collar up and his sleeves rolled. His pants were pegged so tight at his ankles that they must have threatened the circulation in his feet. On the 800 block of George Street, in the Age of the Cool Cat, in the days of ducktail haircuts and pink shirts and suede shoes, Spider Sukoloski was the coolest cat of all.

If I could go back, I would ask Spider if I could touch his hair. I would ask if he would like to trade nicknames, for who would not rather be called Spider than Spit?

The Freilichs did not run the only grocery store on the block. Across the street from Spider's house was Teufel's. Teufel's was about as small as a store could get, no bigger than a row house living room. In fact, it *was* a row house living room before it was converted to a grocery store.

My family did most of its shopping at Freilich's. I bought only two products at Teufel's: candy and Popsicles.

There were two Teufels. One was a stout black-haired woman who managed the store. The other was assumed to be the manager's mother, or grandmother, or great-grandmother, for she was the oldest-looking person any of us had ever seen. We guessed her age at anywhere from ninety to one hundred fifty. She was thinner than a taffy stick. Her scalp looked as if it had been planted with dandelion fuzzballs. I found myself speaking lightly to her for fear that a loud word might blow her over.

No doubt her skin had once been as solidly pink as mine, but much of its pigment had drained away so that she now seemed skinned in waxed paper. Wherever she was left uncovered, you could follow the humped blue tributaries of her circulation. I imagined that her doctor, examining her, could peer, like a tourist on a glass-bottomed boat, right through to her heart and other organs.

The older Miss Teufel was seldom seen. She lived behind a doorway curtain that separated the store from the living quarters. But on occasion when the younger Miss Teufel was away, the older one came out to wait on customers. She sorely tested a kid's patience: It could take forever just to buy a Mounds bar. But I for one did not mind, for watching the old Miss Teufel behind the counter was a fascinating experience. As I stared at the thin, blue-corded hand that passed me the Mounds bar, I wondered, would that be my hand in eighty years? My common sense said yes, but I couldn't quite believe it. The bell above the green-framed screen door tinkled as I happily rejoined the sunshine and the hard reassuring warmth of the sidewalk bricks. Inside, the old woman disappeared behind the curtain.

Henry Doerner lived in the next-to-the-last house on the block—the end of the dead end. Henry was a burly, rambunctious kid. He got into his share of trouble. He didn't take any guff. He was active, feisty, you might even say pushy. When there were games to be played, he was there, in the middle. When there were sides to be chosen, he was there, up front, staring down the chooser.

Maybe that's why Henry Doerner was seldom chosen last. On the other hand, he was never chosen first, for Henry had disabilities. He had been born with one leg too short and an incomplete hand. The short leg required him to wear a special shoe, the sole of which was a leather platform about six inches thick. It leveled off both feet to the ground and made walking, if not graceful, at least possible. The hand was a hand in name only. The wrist tapered to one finger with, as I recall, an extra finger or thumb projecting from where the palm should have been.

And here is the thing: In my memory Henry Doerner is always running. The good leg moves normally, like mine, while the other swings straight outward from the hip, more like an oar than a leg. But he doesn't seem to know, he doesn't seem to care. He just runs. And the rocking chair on his porch is empty, and nobody says, "You can't do that."

The other day I found Henry in one of my high school yearbooks. It's the group picture of Homeroom 49. He stands in the second row, and you can't see the hand or the foot. But you can see the face, and it's pure Henry Doerner: eyes that pierce the camera as if it's the chooser in a pickup game of street football, and a smirk that says, "Go ahead, I dare you not to pick me."

If I could go back and if I could be chooser, I would pick Henry Doerner first.

Among the dead-end population, I count one soul who had no address on George Street. As far as I knew, he had no address anywhere, though he was at home everywhere. He was the hokey-pokey man.

In the warmer months of the year the hokey-pokey

man roamed the streets of town, pushing before him a white wooden cart. The bed of the cart was occupied by a block of ice covered with a dishtowel. Flanking the ice were two rows of bottles containing flavored liquids in a variety of colors that always reminded me of a barbershop shelf.

The hokey-pokey man knew kids. He knew our ways better than we did. As we got older and our routes about town changed, he was always there, ahead of us, waiting: at the dead-end barrier, outside the school, clattering along a random street. Coming upon him, we crowded around the cart.

He went into action. He flipped off the dishtowel, grabbed the ice shaver, clacked it like a castanet, and scraped ice until the scoop was full. He deposited a white snowball into a paper cone and awaited the first order.

"Lime!"

He snatched the lime bottle, shook it, and—presto—bright green snowball.

"Grape!"

"Orange!"

"Lemon!"

I waited till last, thinking about the flavors. I always decided on root beer.

We took off then, relishing the winter on our tongues, giving no thought to the hokey-pokey man. For he was not someone to think about. He was simply there. Where we were.

And then, in time, he wasn't. Though still, on a summer's day, when heat waves dance above the street, I sometimes imagine I see him in the distance, waiting where I have yet to arrive.

And then there were the Seetons. Officially, the Seetons did not live on George Street. The lived on Elm, with their property running perpendicular to the backyards of the Freilichs, the Spinellis, the Corys, and the Sukoloskis.

During my grade-school years, as I have mentioned, I considered Johnny Seeton one of my two best friends, the other being Roger Adelman.

As the years go by, there is something I remember about the Seetons even more than Johnny. It is his mother's whistle. With it she called in however many of her six children were away from the house at dinnertime. She would come out the kitchen door, stand by the fence, and deliver it once, maybe several times. It was not loud. Not nearly as loud as a hot Chevy revving or a kid yapping or a parent scolding. It was a simple two-note whistle. And yet her kids, all of us kids, no matter where we were—Kohn Street, the tracks, Red Hill—we always seemed to hear it.

Dinnertime upon dinnertime, year after year, Mrs. Seeton's whistle reeled in her kids. Sometimes the rest of us came running, too, to our own homes, for a mother's call somehow touches us all. Those two not-very-loud notes echo down to millennium's end and powerfully recall to me a time and a place. A fantasy I have goes like this: Mrs. Seeton returns to her house on Elm Street. The nineties neighborhood kids in bubble-soled sneakers stare at the gray, slow-moving woman whom they do not know. She goes to the backyard, to the old spot by the fence, and she whistles. It's the old two-noter, sounds exactly the way it did in 1955. She doesn't need to whistle again—one is all it takes, because we're already on our way. The nineties kids gape in amazement as we return from our homes and cemeteries around the world—Henry Doerner and Spider Sukoloski and Virginia Cory and Jerry Fox and the Teufels and even little Sharon Freilich, her knees still dirty but not crying anymore—across the Schuylkill River and along the tracks and the path and down the streets and nameless alleyways, all of us one more time heading home on Mrs. Seeton's whistle.

Night

chh

It always began as a solitary chuffing, a sudden explosive snort as if a night beast rising in the distance, down in Conshohocken maybe, had cleared its snout. So faint and faraway was it, so alien, that I usually persuaded myself that it wasn't there. But sooner or later, again, it was.

chh

It seemed to enter my night room from below, catching on the antenna of my bedsprings, running up the coils, whispering through the mattress, the sheet, making an ear of my entire body.

chh

Then the furious flurry.

chhchhchhchhchhchh

My eyes were wide, groping for light, but I could not even see the pillow. I wished I had the nerve to run for the light switch. I wished my room was not at the back of the house, nearest the tracks.

The sound was still far off, along the Schuylkill (SKOO-kul) River, somewhere in the East End, but it had movement now, direction. It was coming. The breath of the night beast beat faster and louder. It was passing the DeKalb Street station now, turning from the river, behind the empty dark Garrick Theater, under the erector set Airy Street bridge, Marshall Street now, between the black and white striped crossing gate, bell tinkling, red light blinking—louder and louder—past the sand place, where I went with my father to bring home a wagonful; past the shoebox-shaped Orange Car store, where my mother could buy a bagful of Florida in February; crossing Elm, bending with the creek—louder, louder, *chhchh chhchhchhchhchh*—behind the ice plant now, Astor Street, the stone piles, the dump—louder still—the iron beast pouring sooty blackness into all the world, creating night—how loud can something be?—coming around the curve at the dead end of Chain CHHCHHCHHCHHCHHCHHCHHCHHCHH CHHCHHCHHCHHCHHCHHCHHCHHCHH— into my room, the bedsprings under me singing like the fiddle strings of Hell...

∗   ∗   ∗

Did it really happen? In morning's comforting sunshine I could never be sure—until I ran my finger along the clothesline or over the yellow face of a pansy in the backyard, and the tiny black particles of grit confirmed: yes, a train—a coal-fired, smoke-belching locomotive—had passed the night before.

Nighttime lent a horror not only to trains but also to garbage. Garbage had status in those days. Garbage was garbage, and trash was everything else. Garbage had a can of its own, basically an oversize metal pail with a lid. The garbage pail could be found in the back of the backyard. To lift the lid off the garbage can was to confront all the horrors of the creepiest movie: dead, rotting matter; teeming colonies of pale, slimy creeping things; and a stench that could be survived only in the smallest whiffs.

Ironically, the garbage can was never more disgusting than the day *after* garbage collection—for the collection was never quite complete. The garbage man would snatch the can from our curbside and overturn it into the garbage truck's unspeakable trough. He would bang it once, maybe twice, against the trough wall. This would dislodge most of the garbage, including a rain of maggots, but not the worst of it, not the very bottom of it, the most persistent, the oldest, the rottenest, the vilest. I held my breath while putting the lid back on. Sometimes I pushed the can all the way to the backyard with my foot.

When garbage met darkness, the potential for horror doubled.

Emptying the garbage after dinner was a frequent chore of mine, but only one particular instance do I remember. My mother had dumped the leftovers into a cake batter bowl and sent me off. The season was winter; it was already dark outside. The light from the back door petered out halfway down the yard, leaving me to moonlight. At the garbage can I went through my usual ritual: I curled my fingers around the metal handle of the lid, took a deep breath, held it, and with an almost audible winching of willpower, yanked the lid off. Careful not to look directly into the can, I overturned the batter bowl. I tapped it against the can to loosen any stragglers—and discovered I had a problem.

Whatever we had had for dinner that night must have been sticky, because half of it was still cling-ing to the bowl. I tapped harder. Still the stuff stuck. Risking breakage, I banged the bowl against the can. Nothing came loose. My chest was getting tight, my lungs demanded breath. In the moonlight I caught a glimpse of white worms. I panicked. I dropped the bowl into the garbage can, slammed down the lid, and raced for the house. I waited until I was inside to gasp for air, as I was sure that the garbage can, open so uncommonly long, must have fouled all outdoors. When my mother asked about the missing bowl several days later, I said I knew nothing about it.

Though night at various times conspired with a locomotive or a garbage can or a pup tent to frighten me, at other times night did not scare me at all.

We used to play a game called outs. It was the major leagues of hide-and-seek games. The kid who was It covered his eyes and counted to a hundred while everyone else ran and hid. If the It kid found you, he yelled "You're out!" and then the two of you were It and went seeking the others, and so on, until all were It but one—the winner.

There were no boundaries. You could hide anywhere. Popular hiding places included the stone piles, Red Hill, alleys, assorted backyards. As if the hiding needed to be made any easier, we always played outs after dark.

My favorite hiding place was behind a stone pile near the creek. I would crouch silently for an hour or more in utter darkness. The dark did not scare me when playing outs. What scared me was being found.

One night I heard the Its coming close to my hiding place. I slipped away down the path to the park and trotted up past the state hospital. I didn't stop until I was more than a mile west of town, in Jeffersonville. By the time I got back home my parents were calling my name down the dark alleys and streets. All the other players were home in bed.

Night was at its best once a week: outdoor movies in the park. After dinnertime and baseball games and Popsicles for dessert, kids from all over town headed for the band shell. Little kids sat in the cement-anchored benches that still form the stage's permanent seats. On the hill behind, older kids pulled up wooden benches or just sat on the grass. One night I must have been thinking I was older than I was. As I made myself at home on a wooden bench on the hill, several teenagers decided that was where they wanted to sit. They lifted the bench at one end, and off I slid to the grass.

The movies were usually in black and white. Occasionally we got through the show without the projector breaking down or the film snapping. More often than not the movie was about Francis the talking mule.

Afterward everyone scattered, across the fields to the East End, North End, West End. We George Streeters walked through the American Legion field and over the granite bridge spanning Stony Creek and turned left. Sometimes we took the dirt path, sometimes the tracks.

On moonlit nights the tracks looked like silver ribbons. Behind me, ahead of me, I could hear the voices of other kids. I could see their dark shadows. Atop the ten-foot clay bluff to the right was the spear field, then the dump, then Red Hill. A bald, packed dome of eraser-colored clay, Red Hill was said to be the home of the Devil, the clay's color coming from the infernal fires burning below. I always looked to see if it was true that at night you could see the hill glowing. Once, I thought, it was.

Always glowing, however, was the dead end, the faint "Welcome home" from the last streetlight. From the path, from the tracks we funneled onto George, the after-dark, midsummer band shell park movie kids. You could always bet that someone would face the row house windows and do his best imitation of a talking mule.

And somewhere beyond the East End a locomotive was moving through the night...

chh

A Family Thing

On the night of May 16, 1936, my mother and father got married. This was three years after Lou Spinelli, nicknamed Poppy, had spotted pretty, dark-haired Lorna Bigler on the dance floor at the Orioles Lodge and said to his friend Babe Richards, "See that girl. That's who I'm going to marry." On the night of their wedding, they were on another dance floor, at the Little Ritz, a nightspot on Route 202 north of town. They were broke, so this was all the honeymoon they would have.

At one point during the evening an announcement was made: A contest would determine the prettiest lady in attendance. My mother doesn't recall the contest procedure, only the result. The winner was the new Mrs. Lou Spinelli. Her prize was a gift certificate to have her portrait done at the Davis Photography Studio.

Four and a half years later, on February 1, 1941, I was born. My brother, Bill, came along four and a half years after that, on July 29, 1945. My mother's wedding-day prize, the framed portrait from Davis Studio, stands today on her bedroom dresser, the center of a triptych flanked by photo portraits of toddlers Bill and me.

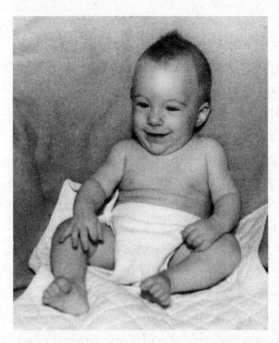

And Jerry makes three. Here I am at three months (1941).

Mothers can get short-changed by memory. My recollections, for example, begin somewhere in my third year. By then some of my best experiences with my mother, some three years' worth of constant daily interaction, were already over. When my mind's recorder finally turned on, it was moments with my father that made the more memorable impressions: trips to high school ball games, backyard baseball, setting up the Christmas crèche. My mother's attentions continued, of course, but they tended to be less obvious, less noticed. They were the background of my life, the everyday care and support that at last came into full recognition when I acquired a family of my own.

The marriage of Louis Anthony Spinelli and Lorna Mae Bigler brought together two heritages: Italian (my father) and Pennsylvania Dutch (my mother).

When I think of my Italian side, I think first of Sundays after church. The four of us would walk—or after 1954, when we got our first car, ride—the four blocks from First Presbyterian to my grandparents' home at 226 Chestnut. It was a row house with porches front and back and a rose arbor and dark polished furniture that made the living and dining rooms feel gloomy to me. The kitchen was where the light and the people and the food were.

Around the kitchen table sat aunts and uncles and cousins and, always at the head, my grandfather, Alessandro "Alex" Spinelli. In front of him was a small glass pitcher of red wine. Before each meal, including a breakfast of cold spaghetti, he drew the wine from his own barrel in the cellar. He was bald and he did not speak English very well and his breath always smelled of garlic and he smoked thin black wicked stogies and his fingers were as thick as sausages. He had labored many years for the Pennsylvania Department of Highways. Later the Borough of Norristown employed him as a street sweeper. Sometimes, riding my bike, I would see him with other old men, pushing a broom along a curb.

That was his job. His love was the "farm," a small patch of vacant land that he rented in the East End.

During the growing months, every day after work, he went to the farm to tend his vegetables. I like to think that, as he put hoe to earth, he sometimes reflected on what to me was the remarkable central fact of his life:

"He came over on a boat all by himself when he was only fourteen years old."

That's how I say it, even now, when describing my grandfather's coming to this country. He was an orphan in Italy. He worked in the olive groves around Naples. An aunt arranged for relatives to meet him in New York, handed him a one-way ticket on a steamship, and off he went, across the Atlantic Ocean, a black-haired teenager, alone, *solo*.

Fifty years later I, a nine-year-old American-born boy, sat at his kitchen table, eating the roast chicken with my fingers because that's how he did it, trying to imagine the bald old man at the head of the table with black hair.

The first course was always salad, as simple as salad gets: lettuce with oil and vinegar. Then came the chicken, then spaghetti and meatballs. My grandmother often made her own spaghetti, rolling out the dough and slicing it into strands with a device that reminded me of a harp. She would spend a whole day nursing the gravy at the stove. (To many Italians, spaghetti sauce is "gravy.") The dessert was often hot chestnuts, roasted on a second stove in the cellar.

As with the Spinellis, a table stands in the center of

my memory of the maternal relatives. In this case the table is not in a kitchen but on a sloping lawn under a huge oak tree. Made of planks laid over sawhorses, the table is very long and is crowded with pickled eggs and cold cuts and potato salad and three-bean salad and lemon meringue pie and dozens of other goodies. The place is my Aunt Isabel and Uncle Ted's home in Phoenixville, Pennsylvania, about ten miles from Norristown. The occasion is the annual family reunion.

In my early years the reunion was, after Christmas, the biggest event on my calendar. It was the only time I got to see Aunt Lizzie and her gang from Highspire, some eighty miles away. Even their names seemed different. There was a Willard and a Juanita and a second cousin exotically named Kendra.

One year there was even more excitement than usual: Uncle Elwood and Aunt Kay drove in from Michigan. I kept staring at my midwestern cousins Bruce, Janey, and Suzie. They might as well have come from Mars. Alas for Aunt Margaret and Uncle Chet and their kids Cindy, George, JoAnne, and Patty, there was no magic of distance. They lived on Chain Street in Norristown, a mere block and a half from 802 George. I barely noticed them.

As a once-a-year event, the reunion became a gauge by which to measure my progress, both physical and social. On the tennis court–size side yard, the uncles always got up a game of softball for the kids. I began as a tiny, grunting fumbler, swinging in vain at the slowest underhand tosses with a bat as big as I was. By the age of ten or eleven, I was clipping the grass with sharp grounders; then line drives to the garage; then, as a seasoned teenage shortstop, long flies into the strawberry patch beyond the trees. But by then the family reunion was no longer number two on my calendar. It had been eclipsed by such happenings as school dances and miniature golf with my friends. The year came when I felt myself too big to participate in the softball game. In college, some years, I did not even attend the reunion.

But home—home is a reunion daily. And I never felt too big for Christmas. Christmas was a Bible thing, of course, and a school-vacation thing and a wrapped-presents thing and a homemade-cookies thing—but most of all, as I look back, it was a family thing.

My parents spent almost nothing on themselves. They bought only the clothes they needed. It was a big deal to treat themselves to a milkshake. They never went to the movies. And yet, for all they gave my brother and me, you'd have thought they were rich. My Christmas gifts came in piles. From Lincoln Logs to the inevitable walnut in the toe of my red felt stocking, I accepted the presents strictly as the objects they appeared to be. Only years later did I realize the truth: the gift was my parents' selfless love.

One Christmas morning it bounced lightly off my

chest as I came down the stairs, and I looked to see my first football wobbling at my feet. Another year it waited for me in the kitchen. I had unwrapped the last present from under the tree, and my father said, "Well, I guess that's it. Looks like you did pretty good this year." And then someone asked me to go to the kitchen for something, and there it was, in front of the sink: a spanking-new cream and green whitewall-tired Roadmaster bicycle. Love leaning on a kickstand.

My mother and father at the beach in 1940, six months before I was born.

Big Brother

When my younger brother became student council president as a ninth grader at Rittenhouse Junior High, I was proud. In the years that followed Bill and I played golf, flung Frisbees, shared friends and cars. We were pals.

But those days were yet to come. During the George Street years, the four-and-a-half-year difference in our ages ruled out being pals. When I was in fourth grade, Bill was in kindergarten; when I was in tenth, he was in sixth. We had different friends, different involvements. Except for two years, we attended different schools. We shared parents and a house, but that was about all.

Because I wasn't paying much attention to him then, my store of memories today is not nearly as well stocked as I would like it to be. I remember him, when he was very young, eating ashes from the coal furnace.

I remember him pilfering my penny collection to buy an ice cream cone.

I remember him as a toddler, packing our first puppy, Spot, into our father's black-domed lunchpail. When this kept happening, Spot was sent off to a family without toddlers.

A few years later along came Lucky (so named because

after the lunchpail puppy, we were lucky to get another), part terrier, part unknown, a pretty mutt, mostly black, with white chest and paws and tip of tail. She was friendly, eager, barely disciplined, which is to say, she was like my little brother. They got along wonderfully.

Our dog Lucky.

I remember feet-fighting in my bed—lying on our backs and flailing our feet at each other. It was just harmless, boy horseplay, but sometimes I carried it far enough so that Bill wound up crying. I think now that in making him cry, I was fabricating an outlet for tender feelings toward my little brother that found no expression in the natural course of events.

I remember Bill getting into trouble more than I, both at home and in school. I secretly admired him for daring to just do things, regardless of consequences.

And I envied him his animation. Well before I entered junior high, I began cooling out. Gone were the days when I would serenade passersby from the gate in my yard or jingle-jangle off to school in my cowboy outfit. I was still friendly, but in a shyer, quieter way. Meanwhile Bill was just lighting up. He was everything I was not: bold and lively and funny. He was a natural mimic and a clown. He had, as the Lloyd Price song went, "Personality."

And that's about it, the extent of my kidhood relationship with my brother, Bill.

Or so I thought.

For something surprising happened, something nice, when I told him I was working on my autobiography. I invited him to jot down any recollections of me that he might have, in case I missed any. Several weeks later he handed me a list of memorable moments. I read it over. I was stunned: I hardly recalled any of them.

He remembers his own hurt feelings when I wouldn't let him ride my tricycle.

He remembers, as a preschooler, how impressed he was that I could read cereal boxes.

He remembers how angry I got when he raided my closet for shirts and when he tangled the strings of my Howdy Doody puppet.

He remembers fearing for me when Raymond Chillano beaned me with a pitch during a Knee-Hi baseball game. And when the same Raymond Chillano, knowing I could not swim, tipped me in my street clothes into the deep end of the pool at the Valley Forge Swim Club. (Raymond was not always so hard on me. In fact, he was one of my best friends.)

He remembers an episode which, at the time, he considered positively historic. I was in the fifth grade at Hartranft Elementary. Bill was in first. Normally we walked the three blocks home for lunch. But on this particular day our mother had to be somewhere else, so she gave me money and told me to take my brother somewhere to eat. We met at noon. We went to a luncheonette a block away. We ordered our lunch, and for a little while Billy Spinelli felt as big as anyone in that place. He was having lunch in a restaurant, not a parent or teacher in sight, off into the world with his big brother. On the way back to school we were chased by bees.

Bill remembers as clearly as I the dirt path by the railroad tracks. He especially remembers one day when I propped him on the bar of my Roadmaster and gave him a lift from the dead end to the park. He remembers feeling the carnival-ride thrill of it. He remembers feeling proud and special. Most of all he remembers feeling safe, his brother's breath in his ear, his brother's arms joining the handlebars in a protective embrace.

Such are Bill's recollections, and after all these years they bumped me over to a new point of view. I have always tended to see our relationship from a single perspective, from my own eyes; that is, Bill as my little brother. Now I see it from a second perspective: myself as his big brother.

I have decided that I like Bill's memories of us better than my own. I especially like the one about the bike ride on the dirt path. I am picturing it now. I am feeling Bill's feeling of safety, and I am feeling the big brother in myself. Maybe, if I keep picturing this memory of Bill's and feeling it for a long-enough time, it will begin to fool me into thinking it is my own.

My brother (left) and me, clowning around at Christmas, 1957. The cigarettes are candy.

Sixteen Things I Wished I Could Do

1. Spit between my front teeth
2. Blast an earsplitting, two-fingered whistle
3. Braid a lanyard with the colorful plastic cord called gimp
4. Drink a quart of milk, or anything, at one sitting (like Roger Adelman)
5. Rock the cradle with my yo-yo
6. Bless myself like a Catholic
7. Tap the side of my nose and blow out a booger
8. Crack a twin Popsicle perfectly in half every time, never to be left with three quarters in one hand and one quarter in the other
9. Bend my thumb backward until it touches my wrist
10. Like cream soda
11. Play clarinet without practicing
12. Stay on my notes when singing harmony
13. Eat hot peppers
14. Hit the curve ball
15. Swim
16. Understand eternity

A Swooner
in Sneakers

Some kids, when no playmates were around, didn't know what to do. I didn't have this problem. There was always exploring, and exploring was best done alone.

The Red Hills, the spear field, the tracks, the path, the dumps—all were sectors to be investigated time and again. But usually my route of exploration followed Norristown's signature waterway: Stony Creek. My territory ranged from two grassy blanket-size islands near the Elm Street bridge to the far end of Elmwood Park, where the creek forked, one branch turning west into the vast farmland of the state hospital, the other meandering north on toward East Norriton Township.

In some places the going was easy, such as the stony flats under the Steriger Street bridge. In others the banks were so steep and near the water that I had to pull myself along with roots for handholds or hop the rocks midstream. The total length was a mile or more— to me it seemed Mississippian—and not an inch along the way, on either side, was unknown to the rubber soles of my black and white hightop Keds.

The zoo toward the far end of the park was, and still is, one of Norristown's treasures, and I visited it often.

But it was near the western edge of the zoo, along the creek, where I came to know creatures unpenned. Squatting over the shallows, I studied schools of minnows in the finger-deep water. I pulled up a rock, and more often than not a crayfish—we called the tiny lobster look-alikes crawfish—scooted briefly into the sunlight and then under another rock. Water spiders skated over the glaring surface while angel-winged dragonflies and neon blue darning needles shimmered above.

Lurking below was something nasty—leeches. Bloodsuckers. They were everywhere, but unseen, unfelt. The only way to observe them was to leave a hand or foot in the water too long. That's what I did once. It was one of the few times I found myself with others at the creek. I was wading—I don't remember why—with my shoes and socks off and my dungarees rolled up, and when I got out, one of the other kids screeched and pointed. I looked down and saw them—black wormlike bloodsuckers clinging to the snow-white skin of my shins. Frantically I scraped them off. Now I was staring at a half-dozen driblets of blood, where the vampires had been dining. Were leeches poisonous? I didn't know, but rattlesnakes were, and I knew from my cowboy days how to handle a snakebite.

I sat on the bank, hoisted a bare leg into the air, and announced, "Okay, you guys, you gotta get the poison out. Start sucking." Suddenly everyone remembered they had to be somewhere else that instant. As they clambered up the banks, I wiped off the blood with my shirt, picked up my socks and sneaks, and walked home as delicately as I could, afraid that if I came down too hard on my bloodless legs, they might crumple. I took a bath and survived the night.

And there were frogs—heard but almost never seen. Try as I might, I was never silent enough to sneak up on them. I knew them only by the watery plops that preceded me as I walked along the creek bank.

There were snakes. Mostly the common garter. But occasionally I chanced upon a truly special snake. Once, down near the Elm Street bridge, I found a large black one sunning on a flat rock. I pinned it behind the head with my stick, picked it up, and took it home. I put it in a two-handled tin picnic box and covered it with perforated cardboard. The next morning the snake was gone. I looked under everything in the house but couldn't find it. Nor could I understand why my mother was so upset. She must have blabbed to the neighbors, because for the next several days panic held the 800 block in its grip. We never found it.

On another day I looked into the creek and saw a small brown and yellow water snake. It was like a jewel set among the sun diamonds sparkling in the water. It was the most beautiful thing I had ever seen, and at first I didn't believe it. When I did, it was gone with the current. I raced downstream, concentrating on shadow patches, for only there was it visible. I caught sight of it once for a moment, then lost it for good. I kept running the bank, searching, searching. The next day I returned to the spot. I stared so long and hard into the creek that once I imagined I saw it, but it was only the rippling, sun-dappled water itself. For the rest of the summer, and the next, as I visited my frogs and crawfish and minnows, I continued to search. And to this day I cannot walk along a stream without hoping for one more glimpse of the beautiful water snake.

And there was my favorite of all—salamanders. I loved the little critters, two inches of wriggle under a rock. Plain brown was the most common coloring. Sometimes I'd find one with an orange stripe. Yellow stripes were the rarest. I became so good at knowing where they lived that I seldom lifted a rock without finding one.

But I loved them wrongly. I wasn't satisfied with simply finding and watching them. I wanted to collect them, as if they were marbles or baseball cards. I remember walking through the park one day with two fistfuls of them and more in my pockets. Once, I brought several home. I turned the black snake's brief abode, the picnic box, into a terrarium: dirt, rocks, water. In went the salamanders. I forget what I fed them. Whatever it was, they didn't eat. One day I found them dead, dried up like pieces of chewed rawhide. I buried them in the backyard, in the earth they should never have been taken from, and kept the lifeless picnic-box terrarium as a reminder of a lesson learned.

When I got my Christmas bicycle, I roamed far beyond the creek. The whole town was now within reach. I rode without destination, with no intent but to look and look and look. To find myself on an unfamiliar street was all the thrill I needed.

I saw the rooftops of row houses stepping down the hills of the East End, like stairways for giants. I coasted the broader avenues of the more affluent North End, amazed to see unattached homes with backyards *and* side yards *and* front yards. I saw the riverbanks of the great Schuylkill—and learned to spell it. I saw the P&W high-speed trolley wobble across the river trestle from Bridgeport to nest at the terminal platform high above Swede Street. In the shadow of the P&W platform I saw the green newsstand with every magazine in the world (or so I thought) and the line of radio taxis, black boxy little Plymouths, one of which was driven by my neighbor, Mr. Seeton. I saw the domed courthouse and the high stone walls of the county prison and the steeple of my church, First Presbyterian, said to be one of the tallest in the land, poking a hole in the sky. I saw the impossibly long (one block!) city hall, where you could get yourself into or out of trouble at one end and buy penny candy at the other. I saw the sprawling red-roofed building of the *Times Herald*, "Montgomery County's newspaper since 1799." I saw and smelled— again—the Adam Scheidt Brewery and the garlicky tang on East Main that came from Linfante's and Lou's, famous for the zep sandwich (salami, provolone, tomato, Bermuda onion, oil, with or without hot peppers), created in Norristown in 1938. I saw the bustling commercial districts of Main Street and West Marshall, with movie theaters—four of them—and restaurants and shops of all sorts and Chatlin's department store, home of the famous fluoroscope.

When you needed new shoes, you went to Chatlin's with your mother. The salesman helped you try them on until you found a pair your mother liked. Then came the best part. The salesman stood up from his fitting stool and said, "Well, why don't we have a look," and off went the three of you to the fluoroscope. It looked something like the big floor console radio in your living room. Six inches up was a step leading to an opening into the interior of the scope. Since you knew the procedure, you didn't even wait for the salesman to say, "Step up." You slid your feet into the opening, and then you had to fight impatience. First the salesman bent over and pressed his face to the goggle-shaped viewer. "Wiggle your toes," he said. You wiggled your toes. He straightened up, nodding. "Plenty of room." Then your mother looked. At last it was your turn. You bent down and scrunched your face to the viewer and there they were—your feet—or rather the skeleton of your feet, your bones, your toe bones wiggling in an eerie green glow. "We'll take them," said your mother, and already you were eager to wear them out so you could come back to Chatlin's and do this again.

Other favorite stops were Block's and Yost's. Block's department store had the only Santa Claus I would talk to at Christmastime. For a long while, I was convinced that Block's was home to the *real* Santa. And though I never bought anything at Yost's, a dry-goods store on the corner of DeKalb and Main, I stopped in occasionally because of a feature I had never seen anywhere else. The selling floor had no cash registers. When someone made a purchase, the salesclerk took the customer's money and stuffed it into a small canister hanging above her head. The canister was threaded onto a heavy string that swooped from the sales counter up through a portal on the second floor. Exactly how and why it all happened was a mystery to me. I only knew that the customer's money was soon zipping up to the second floor, and a minute later down came the canister like a chair on a ski lift with change and receipt. Every counter had its own string to the second-floor portal, so canisters were forever zipping back and forth just out of my reach—and all of this accompanied by tinkling bells. It was a show!

My bike was more than wheels for aimless wandering. It helped me answer many needs.

Did I want to cool off? I coasted through the alley between Kohn Street and Haws Avenue, past the Flavorite ice cream plant.

Was I hungry? I pedaled to a mulberry tree. I knew every one in town. My favorite was in Roger Adelman's backyard. I climbed it often and snacked off the branches, staining my fingers purple.

Did I want a thrill? I rode out to the park zoo, to the top of Monkey Hill. I waited until the road was clear of cars and took off, pedaling hard all the way, down past the monkey cages. My record, according to my speedometer, was forty-five miles per hour, not bad for a single-gear, fat-tired Roadmaster.

Or another kind of thrill? Some days I must have pedaled past Dovie Wilmoth's house on Haws Avenue ten times, hoping that the beautiful platinum blonde would be on the front porch. If she was, I waved and called "Hi, Dovie!" and kept circling the block. Every three minutes: "Hi, Dovie!" She always smiled and waved back.

When I was thirteen, I was old enough to leave town. My Roadmaster took me as far as Valley Forge National Historical Park, about five miles away. I crossed the Schuylkill on the singing bridge, so called for the sound of tires on the steel grate deck. You could see through the deck to the river below. For hours I rode the winding hills past cannon muzzles and monuments and replicated log cabins. Once, I parked my bike and walked into a hillside meadow to lie back and get some sun. When I opened my eyes, hawks were circling overhead. Not trusting them to know I wasn't dead, I got out of there fast.

Sometimes if my planned route for the day took me across the tracks at the dead end, I had to wait for a freight train to pass. I never felt thwarted or impatient about this. In fact, the longer the train the better, and if there were three or four engines, I knew it would be a very long one. By the end of junior high the steam locomotives had given way to diesels. The diesels were neither as terrifying at night nor as exciting in daylight, nor did they leave me with a headful of coal grit.

As the train went by, I counted the cars: boxcars, tankers, flatcars, coal hoppers. By the time the caboose came clicking by, the engines were out of sight and earshot, out beyond the park band shell. I loved the caboose. I was surprised that no one was ever standing at the back rail, coffee mug in hand, watching the world go by.

In those days I was many whats. A kid can be that. Grownups have gone ahead and answered the question: "*What* shall I be?" They have tossed out all the whats that don't fit and have become just one. Teacher. Truckdriver. Businessperson. But a kid is still becoming. And I, as a kid alone, was free to be just about anything.

So many careers came and went through me: salamander finder, crawfish annoyer, flat-stone creek skipper, cedar chest smeller, railroad car counter, tin can stomper, milkweed blower, mulberry picker, snowball smoother, paper bag popper, steel rail walker, box turtle toucher, dark-sky watcher, best-part saver. They didn't last long, these careers of mine, but flashed into and out of existence like mayflies. But while they employed me, I gave them an honest minute's work and was paid in the satisfactions of curiosity met and a job well done.

When I went roaming by myself on foot or bike, I discovered more than water spiders and foreign neighborhoods. I discovered myself. By myself, not boxed in by rules of play, I was free to think, to wonder, to swoon.

That's what I did sometimes: I swooned, just thinking about things. Like time. Like space. I tried to imagine, tried to grasp the speed of light. One hundred eighty-six thousand miles per *second!* And how about those stars up there? The ones I saw when the sky turned the color of my dungarees. I had heard that these were only the closest ones, visible from earth. I had heard that there were billions and billions more too far away to see, that they went on and on and on until the end of the universe. I tried to imagine zooming out past the last stars and looking around—at what? What does the end of the universe look like? And what about time? What about *before* time?

Thoughts like these did not come to mind as I flipped baseball cards with Spider Sukoloski or played street football with Jerry Fox or gunslingers with Johnny Seeton. They presented themselves behind closed eyes on hillside meadows and during the long lazy wait for a box turtle to cross the path. The questions were as elusive as the answers, as delicate as a dragonfly's wing. They gave me goosebumps. They made me dizzy. I swooned in my sneakers.

A Little Stiff from Swimming

But I did not read. Not books, anyway. Now, cereal boxes—that was another story. Every morning I pored over boxes of Wheaties and Cheerios at the breakfast table. I looked forward to new cereals as much for a change in reading material as for a change in breakfast fare.

And comics. I read them by the hundreds.

Mostly I read cowboy and war comics. I bought them at corner stores and newsstands. Then when I was twelve, I got serious. I decided the comic should come to me. I got my first subscription: *Bugs Bunny*. Once a month, accompanied by the metallic flapping of the front door mail slot, the postman delivered Bugs's latest adventures to me.

My favorite comic character of all, however, was neither man nor rabbit. In fact, I'm still not sure what it was. All I know is that it was called the Heap, and it looked something like a haystack. The Heap never spoke, and the reader never saw it move, but the Heap appeared on the scene when people were having problems. Somehow or other the Heap managed to solve the problem, though it never got credit. As far as most of the people knew, it was just another haystack in the field.

Of course, I read the newspaper comics too. While I never missed "Dick Tracy," "Little Lulu," and "Mandrake the Magician," my favorite of all was "Alley Oop."

Another part of the newspaper got my attention as well: sports.

Mostly I read the sports pages of the *Times Herald*. I especially liked the clever writing of sports editor Red McCarthy in his daily column. Until then I had thought there was only one English language—the language I spoke and heard in the West End of Norristown. I was happily surprised to discover that there was more than one way to say something, that the words and their arrangement could be as interesting as the thing they said.

From April to September in the Sunday *Philadelphia Inquirer*, I read the major league baseball batting statistics. They were printed in small type in a long box, row after row of numbers and names, hundreds of them— every player in the majors. To the non-baseball fan, they were as boring as a page in a phone book. I loved it. I wallowed in the numbers. What was Ted Williams's batting average this week? Stan Musial's? Richie Ashburn's? Was Ralph Kiner still the leader in home runs? Who had the most RBIs? Did Mantle have a shot at the Triple Crown? Or Mays? It was like peeking at a race once every seven days, watching the lead change places from week to week.

Cereal boxes, comics, baseball stats—that was my reading. As for books, I read maybe ten of them, fifteen tops, from the day I entered first grade until graduation from high school. I remember reading a few Bobbsey Twins adventures, and in junior high, sports stories about Chip Hilton, a fictional high school hotshot athlete. I read *The Adventures of Robin Hood*, a Sherlock Holmes mystery, and *Kon-Tiki*, the true story of a man who crossed the Pacific in a raft. That's about it.

Why didn't I read more?

I could blame it on my grade school, which had no library. I could blame it on the curriculum, which limited my classroom reading to "See Dick run. See Jane run. See Spot do something on the rug." I could blame it on history, for enrolling me in life and school before the time of book fairs and author visits. I could blame it on my friends, because like me, the only books they read were comic books.

But I can't do that.

It's always handy to blame things on one's parents, but I can't do that either. My father had his books on display in the dining room. Thirty times a day I passed his collection of histories and Ellery Queen mysteries. Some of my earliest memories are of my mother reading to me, stories like *Babar* and *The Little Engine That Could*. My parents steered me in the right direction.

And the fact is, on those few occasions when I actually did read a book, I enjoyed it. Yet for some reason I would not admit this to myself. Instead of saying, Hey, that was good, that was fun, I think I'll read another— I would dump my baseball glove into my bike basket and head out the path to the Little League field, and months would go by before I picked up a book again. Reading a book was for times when I was totally bored and lacking anything else to do.

And what about words, which, packed together, made up a book as cells made up my body? I liked them. Yet this was such a naturally occurring, unachieved sort of thing that if someone had asked me in those days, "Do you like words?" I probably would have shrugged and blithely answered, "No."

Still, whether I knew it or not, words were claiming me. When I visited Hartenstine Printing, where my father worked as a typesetter, I saw words being created letter by letter, one thin slug of lead at a time.

Once, in a comic book, someone with a bad heart was described as having a bum ticker. That tickled me to no end. I kept whispering "bum ticker" to myself for days.

Except for the Heap, my favorite comic book characters were Bugs Bunny and Daffy Duck. I liked them as much for their words as their ways. For me, the highlight of a scene was not what happened, but what Bugs or Daffy said about what happened. This is probably why Mickey Mouse never much appealed to me. His speech was too bland for my taste.

When I was eleven or twelve, my mother and I laughed for months over a corny old vaudeville joke that I kept asking her to repeat. She gave the joke a local twist. It went like this:

Man goes to the beach for a vacation. Goes into the water. When he comes out, he sees a lady sitting next to his blanket.

He says, "Hi, I'm a little stiff from swimming."

She says, "Hello, I'm a secretary from Norristown."

(I'm laughing again.)

Occasionally I had to look up a word in the dictionary. Sometimes my eye would stray to the surrounding words. Invariably it stopped at an interesting one, and I read the definition. In one such instance I discovered that I was a gossoon. I clearly remember two feelings attached to these moments: (1) surprise that a dictionary could be so interesting, and (2) a notion to sit down and look through more pages. I never did.

And then of course there was my success in spelling.

All of these items were indicators of an early leaning toward language, but I failed to see them as such. The tickle of a rabbit's wit, the rattle of alphabet in a compositor's drawer—they simply took their place among the Popsicles and penknives and bike tires of my days.

With one exception.

In sixth grade our teacher assigned us a project: Make a scrapbook of Mexico. I found pictures of Mexico in *National Geographic* and other magazines and pasted them in my scrapbook, for which my father made a professional-looking cover at the print shop. Then I did something extra. It wasn't part of the assignment. I just did it.

I wrote a poem.

Three stanzas about Mexico, ending with a touristy come-on: "Now, isn't that where you would like to be?" I wrote it in pencil, longhand, my best penmanship, on a piece of lined classroom paper. I pasted it neatly on the last page of my scrapbook and turned in my project.

Several days later my mother walked the three blocks to my school. She met with my teacher, who told her she did not believe that my poem about Mexico was my own work. She thought I copied it from a book. (Hah! If she only knew how few books I read, and never one with poetry.) I was suspected of plagiarism.

I don't know what my mother said to her, but by the time she walked out I was in the clear, legally at least. Five years would pass before I wrote another poem.

Staying in the Lines

I was neat.

How neat was I? Say I had to cut a rectangle out of a piece of paper. First I would measure a perfect shape with my ruler, then draw it with a sharp pencil. Then with my scissors I would cut it out. But not *just* cut it out. I would cut precisely along the right edge of the pencil line, or precisely along the left edge, or I would split the line in half and cut precisely right down the middle. Consistently, all the way around the rectangle.

In seventh grade at Stewart Junior High, I astonished my shop teacher, Mr. Rohn, with the precision of my mechanical drawings and the perfection of my hand-lettering.

That same year I won numerous Palmer Method penmanship certificates and was declared the outstanding boy penmeister.

Every Eastertime the merchants of the West End shopping district—three blocks on Marshall Street—sponsored a coloring contest. Every day for two weeks line drawings—coloring-book-type pictures—were printed in the *Times Herald*. Each business had its own picture. Kids were invited to cut out the pictures, color them, and deposit their entries in boxes in the stores.

Unlike most kids, I did not use crayons. I used colored pencils. My frequently sharpened points never—*never*—strayed outside the lines. And my colors were right, too. No green sky or red grass for me.

For me, staying inside the lines was more than a color-the-picture matter.

Give me a direction, I followed it. Put a rule in front of me, I obeyed it. In twelve years I never stayed after school for detention. Once, though, I came close. It happened in the spring of ninth grade. Our homeroom teacher, Miss Busch, announced that our lockers would be reviewed for neatness. Since I kept my locker neat at all times, there was nothing for me to tidy up.

The next morning as the students entered Homeroom 213, we looked to the blackboard for the names of those whose lockers failed to pass muster. Shockingly, my name was among them. The punishment, besides cleaning up the offending locker, was detention.

I told Miss Busch there must be a mistake. She said there wasn't. I said I wouldn't be there for detention. It was the only time I ever talked back to a teacher. She said I'd be sorry.

After school that day, as usual, I went to baseball practice. When I arrived at school the next morning, I discovered I was no longer on the team. Nor was I homeroom president. I was stripped of every office and association.

My locker may have been tidy, but suddenly my life was a mess. One day of watching my backup shortstop was enough. I couldn't stand it. I apologized to Miss Busch, and the picture of my life fell back into place.

I loved routine, repeatedness. To do the same thing twice was to establish a personal tradition. In other words, where there were no lines, I drew my own. I stepped inside and stayed there—cozy, safe.

Summer Saturdays, for example. In the morning I walked a mile from George Street to the YMCA. There I played Ping-Pong in the game room with Lee Holmes, Ralph Cottman, and others. Then a screen and projector were brought out, the lights turned off, and we all settled in to watch a black and white movie, usually a Tarzan adventure.

After the movie I walked down to Main Street, past Block's department store, past the Norris Theater, to Texas Hot Wieners. The best hot dogs in town were sizzling right there in the front window, daring each passerby not to come in. I sat at the counter and placed my order, always the same: hot dog with mustard and chopped onions, and chocolate milk. I've had a lot of wimpy hot dogs since then, hot dogs so soft you can't feel your teeth go through them, so mushy with fat and cereal you could almost drink them with a straw. Not Texas Hot Wieners. They had spunk. They fought back.

By now it was one o'clock. Across the street I went to the Garrick Theater and the Saturday matinee double feature—cowboy movies plus a Flash Gordon or Captain Midnight serial.

Hours later I emerged blinking in the late-afternoon sun. I walked home along Markley Street, past the sweet-smelling Wonder Bread plant, the sidewalk dusty with flour, past the *Times Herald*, over the Markley Street bridge that spanned Stony Creek. I always stopped at the bridge railing to look for sunfish in the sparkling water below. Only when I spotted one would I continue my journey homeward.

Every summer Saturday. The same thing.

Needless to say, I was well acquainted with perfect attendance in school. Most years went by without my missing a day.

When I walked, I trained myself to keep my feet pointed straight ahead, not pigeon-toed or splayed outward.

I even fantasized about neatness. I imagined our house had been selected for a visit by President Eisenhower. I saw myself going from room to room putting everything precisely in its place. On the racks in the bathroom the corners of the towels came together perfectly.

In another fantasy I set out to tidy up the world. Anything I couldn't fix with hedge trimmers and lawn mower I paved over with asphalt. By the time I was finished, the

Amazon jungle looked like the flower beds and crewcut lawns of the North End of Norristown.

I spread my peanut butter evenly over my bread.

I never said bad words (unless you count "poop").

I hardly ever laughed out loud.

As I said, I was neat. And though I did not think of it this way, I believe that what I was actually trying to do was to become perfect.

Funny thing: For all my neatness, my sharp pencil points, my devotion to the right side of the line, I never won the West End shopping district coloring contest. Every year I tried harder than before, tried to be even neater, and still I lost. I couldn't figure out why.

Wasn't neatness enough? Wasn't perfection possible?

No, said my yo-yo. Often I had what seemed to be a perfect day—100 on a spelling test, winning touchdown in a pickup game, a new haircut—only to come home and find knots in my yo-yo string. I began to think the string had a mind of its own. I imagined it waiting until I wasn't looking, then rising up like a cobra and looping itself into knots. My paranoia seemed confirmed one morning when I awoke to find knots that I could have sworn were not there when I went to bed.

When I was eleven and twelve, I played Biddy basketball, the equivalent of Little League baseball. In my final year I made the all-star team, but not because I was a great scorer. The most points I ever scored in a game was twelve, and usually it was half that. I think I made the all-stars as much for what I did not do as for what I did. That is to say, I did not make mistakes.

Playing the guard position, I dribbled a lot and passed a lot. But these were relatively risk-free ventures. Shooting was where the risk was, and I rarely took more than five shots in a game. I wasn't a bad shooter, but each shot I missed discouraged me from taking more. At home after each game, I neatly entered into a notebook my statistics: assists, shots taken, shots made, fouls. Of course I hardly ever committed a foul. And because I played the game so carefully, I never found out how good a basketball player I might have become. Too late I learned that neatness does not serve all endeavors equally well, that what is good for penmanship is not necessarily good for basketball.

A willingness to take risks, to color outside the lines, was slow in coming to me. Some stubborn idea of perfection deterred me from fully extending myself in simple, pure participation. I was too afraid to fail. I did not appreciate the value of a mess.

Not that I wasn't given the chance. Looking back, I can see now that that's what the school-locker incident was: an opportunity to grow beyond my own self-imposed limits. And for one day, I did. Falsely accused of having a disorderly locker, I was properly outraged. I defied my teacher. I refused to submit to injustice. I turned my back on detention. I charged across the line. I became a new me.

Then came the consequences—banishment from the baseball team, from all offices. Did I rise up and cry, "Punish me if you will! I don't care! I will never capitulate to this injustice"? Did I finish out the year in noble exile, stripped of all honors? Did I stand up for what I knew was right?

No.

I caved in. I apologized for protesting an unjust verdict. My life was reinstated. Order was restored, the mess was cleaned up. I was back inside the lines. Once again I was the old familiar me.

Yet even as I publicly conformed in word and deed, a contrary tendency was forming within me. It showed briefly in sixth grade when I wrote the unassigned poem on Mexico. It showed in my neatness fantasies— not in the subject matter but in the mere act of fantasizing. It showed in my swooning wonderment over the endlessness of the sky at night.

And it showed most commonly in my own version of the Garrick Theater's double features. When an event in my life—say, a baseball game—was over, it was not really over. For that night in bed I would relive it in my head. I would again see the vivid colors and hear the voices and feel the feelings, and the reliving would be, in its own way, as real to me as the first time around. Sometimes it was even better. Sometimes I couldn't wait for the event to be over and bedtime to arrive so that I could play it back.

As I have said, if you had asked me what I would grow up to be, I would have answered, "A baseball player." But even as I oiled the deep, fragrant pocket of my Marty Marion glove and taped the hickory handle of my thirty-three-ounce bat, I was unknowingly developing the tool of another trade. The urge to write a poem, to daydream, to ruminate, to wonder, even my tolerance of solitude—all became components of a bearing that I would never have guessed would fit me so well, an aptitude that thrives on disorder, that welcomes green sky and red grass, that serves neither master nor homeroom teacher, that respects no line or limit. I speak, of course, of imagination—a gift that, like my Roadmaster on that Christmas morning, waited in another room for my discovery.

Dr. Winters'
Finger

There was one line in my life that I did cross freely, frequently, and deliberately. This line ran from one end of town to the other and it had a name.

DeKalb Street.

That is its name in Norristown. Elsewhere it is known as U.S. Route 202, running from Delaware up to Maine. DeKalb Street came off the bridge across the Schuylkill and ran south to north past the Reading Railroad station, past Hartenstine Printing where my father worked, past Yost's Dry Goods and Sames Book Store and First Presbyterian and city hall and the YWCA and St. Patrick's Church and on past the large stone homes of the North End and across Johnson Highway and out of town.

But DeKalb Street divided more than east from west in Norristown. It also divided black from white. With few exceptions, African Americans lived to the east of DeKalb Street. So did many Italian Americans, including my grandparents and, for a while—at 224 Chestnut—me.

My first memory of a black person dates to that time, when I was three or four. My mother took me with her to the dentist one day. The dentist was Dr. Winters. Dr. Winters was black. His office was in the East End.

The story as I have sometimes told it goes like this: My mother has her dental work done while I sit off to the side. When Dr. Winters is finished, I decide I'm jealous of all the attention my mother has been getting. I want some, too. So the dentist hoists me into the chair, tells me to open wide, and checks me over.

In truth, my mother and I have no specific recollection of why I wound up in the dentist's chair. My memory is clear, however, on one thing: Dr. Winters' finger in my mouth. I can feel it, I can see its dark brownness. I notice that it is a color different from my own, but that's all there is to it, a flat, casual observation. What I feel is the rightness of that thick and hard and smooth and gentle and expert finger. My mouth yields naturally to it, seems to recognize that this is the way of things.

Dr. Winters never actually worked on my teeth, but to this day the sense and touch of that "examination" is inscribed vividly in my memory.

Though I lived in the East End for several years, I had no black friends or playmates. Halfway through first grade we moved to George Street, where everyone was white. In my class at Hartranft Elementary there was only one black student, a girl, Viola Fisher. For six years Viola Fisher barely said a word, barely moved. Though her color made her conspicuous at Hartranft, her demeanor rendered her all but invisible. Socially speaking, we white students did not see Viola Fisher.

Looking back today, I can easily imagine Viola Fisher's discomfort. I imagine she often wished she could attend Washington School, deep in the East End, where almost all the students were black. I imagine she was afraid of us. And that's ironic, because in grade school, in my experience, fear went the other way: *we* were afraid of *them*. At least I was.

One day when I was nine, a black boy about my age walked up to me on a school playground, made a fist, and clipped me on the tip of my chin. *Thock.* That was all. The punch did not hurt me, at least not my chin. Nor did the boy seem interested in continuing. Perhaps he simply wanted to make some point. Perhaps it was something he needed to do, as several years later I "needed" to clip Joey Stackhouse on the chin. Whatever, at that moment my fear of black kids felt confirmed. I turned from the boy, trotted over to a nearby tree, knelt in the surrounding dirt, dumped out my bag of marbles, and began shooting mibs.

The fear that steered me through streets and playgrounds came from a perception for which I had no words, a perception I did not question. It said that black people were different from me in ways that went beyond skin color. It did not tell me how they were different, just that they *were* different. It is not clear how I acquired this information. I don't believe it came from home, yet somehow, from the world around me, I absorbed it.

There were signs everywhere. I saw, I heard, but that was all. I did not much think. I did not question.

Crayola crayons came in small and large boxes. The large box contained a pale pink-orange color called flesh. I did not often use it. After all, the pages of the coloring book were white, so it was easier to simply leave faces untouched. I never asked, "*Whose* flesh?"

The most popular private trash collector in town was a black man. He worked hard. In the summer especially he became thirsty. Sometimes he would ask a business client if he could get a drink of water from their faucet, and he would show the glass that he always carried with him. He was widely commended for this. I never asked him, "What do you think would happen if you didn't bring your own glass?"

I once attended a picnic of mixed races. Things were going along normally when, with the picnic only half over, I suddenly noticed that all the black people were gone. I did not run after them and call out, "Wait! Why are you leaving early?"

When my father took me to high school basketball games, I noticed that most of the black people sat in one section of the bleachers. I never asked, "Why do they always sit together?" Or, "Why do *we* always sit together?"

I saw these little separations in a hundred places and a hundred ways, and never once did I say, "Why?"

Though I had neither wit nor grit to ask such questions, sometime in grade school my point of view began to change. It happened when I gave up cowboys and soldiers and turned to sports.

Sports, especially Little League baseball and Biddy basketball, brought me into a new kind of contact with African-American kids. Within the structure of organized games they ceased to be black and I ceased to be white. Instead we were teammates or opponents, identified by the color of our uniforms, not of our skin. The Red Sox. The Green Sox. The Colts. The Wolves. The fear in the streets did not follow me onto sandlots and hardwood courts.

On summer mornings we came from the East End and the West End to play on the Little League field by Stony Creek. In the afternoon the scene switched to the park basketball court. It was during those long hot days that I began to question everything I'd been taught by the countless separations between black and white in Norristown. And I came to see that color was the only difference, as people, between us. And that's all it was: merely a difference, not an exclusion.

One of my best friends was Louis Darden, who was black. At one time or another Louis and I played on football, basketball, and track teams for Hartranft Elementary and Stewart Junior High. Louis was a happy-go-lucky guy. He was truly a player, not a worker, of games.

As the fastest boy at Hartranft, Louis was entered in the hundred-yard dash at the Norristown grade-school track-and-field meet. Something happened in that race which, even more than my own winning of the fifty-yard dash, remains as my most vivid memory of that day. The starter's gun went off and the six runners bolted down the cinder track. At the halfway mark it was clear that Louis was not going to win. The runner from Gotwals, Robert Lee, was well ahead of the pack. But Louis was still in the hunt for a second- or third-place medal, and in the grandstand I stood and cheered him on. About twenty yards from the tape, Louis looked to his left and right at his cinder-churning competitors, and suddenly he eased up, he slowed to a kind of whimsical prance, he threw his arms into the air and as the others raced over the finish line, he laughed.

I was stunned. I was outraged. Not that he lost, not even that he gave up. It was his attitude that bothered me most, lah-di-dahing twenty yards from the finish line. How dare he race and not care! How dare he lose and laugh! Didn't he know this was serious business? The championships of all the grade schools in Norristown, Pennsylvania! I—who took my sports, my baseball cards, my spelling, my life so seriously—could neither understand nor swallow it. Before all the world Louis Darden had disgraced himself. And what was he doing about it? He was laughing.

Two years later it was I who backed off and Louis who cared.

After school one day a group of us were playing basketball under a telephone-pole hoop outside Roger Adelman's backyard. In addition to Roger and me, Louis Darden, Joe Portano, and a few others were there. It fell to Joe Portano to guard me, and that was a mismatch, for Joe was not much of a basketball player. Big and burly, he was more at home in the trenches of a football game. A mouse by comparison, I scooted around him and scored at will. I didn't much note his increasing frustration until suddenly he kicked the ball into the weeds and came after me. He shoved me in the chest with the open palms of both hands. I went reeling backward. I regained my balance, and he slammed into me again, growling and scowling. And then Louis was between us, shoving Joe Portano in the chest, sending him backward, sending him away. There was no laughing this time, no lah-di-dahing, no messing around. For once Louis Darden was all business. Louis Darden, who hadn't cared about winning for himself, made sure that I didn't lose.

The boy who beat Louis in that hundred-yard dash, Robert Lee, was the same boy who'd clipped me on the chin when I was nine. I'm sure he had forgotten the incident long before we met in high school and became friends. By then my views were quite different. I was beginning to ask questions, though not yet out loud. And as was my habit, I fantasized.

I imagined Robert Lee and me back on that playground, and I imagined him again coming up to me and socking me. Only this time I don't turn away. This time I do not fear his color. This time I know that we are the same, and fear is replaced by respect, and because I respect him as I respect myself, I sock him back. And the two of us stare wide-eyed at each other, and then we nod and shake hands and go off together to shoot some marbles.

Louis Darden, 1954.

God and Garfield
Shainline

In 1994 I received a letter from an elementary school reader that ended with this:

"I got my whole life planned out. First I'm gonna grow up. Then I'm going to college. Then off to the air force we go. Then I retire to Hawaii. Then I die. Does that sound good to you?"

What it sounded like was something I myself might have written once upon a time. Except that I would probably have closed with "And then I go to heaven."

Heaven as I saw it would be the logical extension of my perfect attendance in Sunday school. As a military career can be deciphered from parade ribbons on a uniform, so my attendance record could be read on the lapel of my best sport coat. It started with a round blue pin, my reward for attending Sunday school thirteen weeks in a row—one fourth of a year. After twenty-six Sundays in a row, I turned in the blue pin for a red one. Another pin change occurred at week thirty-nine, and then after fifty-two straight Sundays—one year—I received a white pin, mine to keep forever.

A second year of perfect attendance ("perfect" in this case meaning at least forty-eight out of fifty-two

Sundays) earned me a gold wreath to go around my white pin. Then came the bars—red, white, blue—one per year, hanging from the wreathed pin like a little ladder. In time the proof of my perfection was nearly as long as my lapel.

Sometime in junior high, probably at a school dance, I became self-conscious of my Sunday school decorations, and from then on they stayed home.

By then, too, my image of God was changing. Earlier I had pictured God as an old fellow, bearded, abiding somewhere beyond the whipped cream fluffiness of that cumulus cloud out over Elmwood Park. Except for God's magical abilities, I would have been hard put to tell you the difference between him and the last surviving Civil War veteran.

As I got older, that view began to break up, to warp and fuzz over like a TV picture assaulted by interference. I waited and waited for the picture to clear, I fiddled with the dials, but I could not restore God's image to the clarity of my early years. They had taken God out of the coloring book and told me he was not an old man after all but a spirit, that he was not *there* or *there* but everywhere, not *then* or *then* but beyond all whenevers.

Like most kids, I did not take readily to abstraction. Whether tin cans or gods, I felt most comfortable with presences that I could see, could touch, could kick if need be, could hear skittering along a sidewalk. I still spoke to God every night in my prayers, but my sense of a listener had dissipated. How do you speak to both the other side of your pillow and the other side of the Milky Way? I blew my prayers like bubbles into the air and trusted them to winds I could not feel. Hiding by the stone piles during the nighttime games of outs, I gazed into the starry sky and searched the constellations for my Sunday school lessons, and perhaps when I was swooning over time and galaxies, I was swooning over God as well.

If I ever came close to meeting God, I think it was not in the stars but in Garfield Shainline.

For a man with such a big name, Garfield Shainline was quite little, not as short as a dwarf, but almost. As a thirteen-year-old, I was already taller than he. It was said that he shopped for clothes in children's departments. His white hair was crewcut. Tufts of black hair sprouted from his ears and from around a pea-size mole on his chin.

He worked at the YMCA in a wire mesh–enclosed compartment in the locker room. If you were taking a shower, you stopped at the cage and he handed you a small bar of white soap. I'm sure he had other duties, but to most of the boys in town, who never knew his name, that was the sum of who he was: the tiny old man at the Y who hands you soap.

But he was something else, too. When I was a teenager, he was my Sunday school teacher. Every Sunday morning we sat around a heavy round table in the

Christian Education Room of First Presbyterian: Garfield Shainline, Teddy Barrett, David Allen, Jay John, Douglas Nagy, me. We barely listened to him as we snickered and whispered and generally behaved like the immature adolescents that we were. We invented silly questions for him. We dared one another to yank out one of his mole hairs. Our favorite pastime was to pretend to drop something so that we had to bend under the table to retrieve it, there to behold the sight that brought us unending mirth: Garfield's tiny feet, shod in tiny brown leather hightop shoes, dangling in the air like a five-year-old's.

Each session concluded with an around-the-table prayer. Sometimes after the usual petitions for world peace and food for the hungry, someone would say, "And God bless Garfield and give him vitamins so he can grow and touch the floor."

Occasionally Garfield gave us a mild scolding, but mostly he smiled good-naturedly or ignored our nonsense and went on with the important thing, the lesson. No matter how we treated him one Sunday, he was glad to see us the next. Undeserving as we were, we received only the highest recommendations in his prayer.

Upon reaching high school age, we left Garfield behind for another teacher. One day someone told us he was ill and in the hospital and would love to have a visit from his boys, as he called us.

I thought about going to see him, but there were too

many other things to deal with: sports, grades, girls, friends. When I heard that he had died, I did not think much about it. I did not attend his funeral. Nor, I believe, did the others. But deep inside, even as I pretended to ignore my feelings, I sensed that something had changed forever. I pictured him in that hospital bed, waiting day after day for a visit that never came, and I knew—I *knew*—that in his final conscious hours, despite it all, he posted to heaven not a bitter thought about his boys.

Garfield Shainline has been long forgotten by most. Even my mother does not remember him. But I do. Oh, yes, I do. In these many years I have wished many times for him a second death, for myself a second chance. And still today he grows and grows inside of me, Garfield Shainline, the little man who hands you soap, and I have come at last to learn what he never knew he taught, that Garfield Shainline was not the teacher but the lesson.

Girls

The instant my mother saw my face, she gasped. It flashed through her mind that I had suddenly contracted measles or scarlet fever or some such red and rashy affliction. She pulled me farther into the light of the living room. It wasn't a disease—it was lipstick, red lippy patches of it all over my face. I had just come home from a birthday party at Nona Norris's. I explained that we had played some sort of game—the exact nature of which I don't recall—that resulted in all the girls mobbing one boy and smooching him dead with their red, oh-so-grownup lipsticky lips. My mother told me to go upstairs and wash it off. She remembers almost wishing it *had* been measles. I was seven years old. And I already had a girlfriend.

Judy Brooks.

Judy Brooks lived in a yellow-brick front-porch twin house half a block up the street, at 718 George. She wore her brown hair in pigtails. She could tie a dress bow behind her back. She jump-roped double Dutch. She could scream high enough to make dogs howl. She played jacks and handclap games. She whispered and giggled a lot.

We began our relationship in first grade, after I entered Hartranft Elementary partway through the year. I don't remember how I determined that she was my girlfriend, only that I thought of her that way, and that if someone said to me, as adults do, "Do you have a girlfriend?" I would say, "Yes." And the adult would say, "Who?" And I would say, "Judy Brooks."

There wasn't much more to it than that. As a romance, it could be better described by what did not happen as by what did. We did not hold hands, we did not kiss, we did not walk to school together, we did not even talk much to each other. I did, however, accompany her parents to a dance recital that she participated in. And one Saturday morning I went with her to her dentist, Dr. Wenof on Marshall Street. I remained behind in the waiting room while she bravely followed the nurse out of sight. Minutes later I heard her scream. I tensed. I fretted. Was she screaming for me? What were they doing to her? Was it...The Needle? Should I charge in and rescue her? I stewed for another minute or two, then returned to my comic book.

When I say we did not kiss, I mean there was no *we* kissing. Never did she kiss me while I, at the same time, kissed her back. But once, *I* kissed *her*. Whether I wanted to or not.

One day when we were ten, Judy Brooks and I were on the other side of the tracks, near the creek. I was showing her the best kind of rocks to find salamanders under when Eddie Carcarey showed up. This was not good news. Eddie Carcarey and I had been having our problems. They had begun about a year before when I decided to organize a gang and invited Eddie to join. Eddie was one tough hombre, and I figured he would give the gang some muscle. He joined but then refused to abide by the gang's only rule: to call me Captain. So I kicked him out. He retaliated by marching into our backyard in broad daylight and knocking over my mother's basket of clothespins.

And now Eddie Carcarey was coming toward Judy and me with mischief in his eyes.

"Pick her up," he said.

"Huh?" I said.

"Pick her up. Pick her up." His red hair and freckles flared with menace.

Judy was terrified. I imagine I looked terrified to Eddie as well, but in fact I wasn't. I had never picked up a girl before. I had never even *thought* about picking up a girl, but now that I was being ordered to do so, it didn't seem like such a bad idea. In fact, considering that the girl to be picked up was Judy Brooks, it seemed like a darn good idea.

I had seen plenty of pickups on television and in the movies, mostly cowboys hoisting ladies in long dresses who had fainted or sprained their ankle. So I figured I knew the basic move.

"Okay," I said, trying to sound scared.

While Judy stood rigid as a tree trunk, I positioned myself behind her and went through my pre-pickup sequence: spread and plant the feet, crouch, right arm behind her knee, left arm across her back, and—lift. In the movies the lady always came up smartly from the ground, as if she were on a swing, as if she were light as a balloon. It didn't go quite that way for me.

When I lifted, Judy's feet came up all right, as high as my shoulder, but the rest of her went down. Her head was around my knees, and now she was sliding toward the ground, her hand groping for my belt. I quickly dropped to one knee and propped her back against the other.

Eddie Carcarey sneered, "You're weak as an ant."

Maybe so, but I wasn't through yet. Driven not by Eddie Carcarey's sneer but by visions of Lash La Rue and Tex Ritter and how they would have done it, I pulled Judy into my butter pickle biceps, I squatted like a weightlifter, I took a deep breath, I heaved and grunted, and I picked her up. It wasn't a classic—her head and knees were high while her rear end sagged in the middle, giving her a V-shape. My arms turned to stone, my knees buckled under me. But I thought hard of Lash and Tex, and I held it for a good five seconds before I let her down.

"Now kiss her," Eddie said.

Good thing that's what he said, because the only part of my body not in muscular shock was my lips. I gave her a quick peck on the cheek, and that, to my recollection, was the first time I ever kissed a girl.

Eddie Carcarey trotted off, no doubt pleased with himself for forcing me to perform two distasteful acts.

That was the year Judy Brooks broke up with me. Well, strictly speaking, she didn't break up with *me*, she broke up with everyone. She announced that she was through with boys, she hated them all—"you all," I believe, is how she put it. I tried to find a loophole, but no matter how I looked at it, I was a boy, I was one of "you all." For the first time since first grade, I was single.

With a grim, gritting vengeance, I decided to retaliate by hating all girls, which I did successfully for three or four weeks—or was it three or four minutes? In any case, by sixth grade I had another girlfriend.

Bobbi Garber.

Like Judy Brooks, Bobbi Garber lived in the 700 block of George Street. She was one of three beautiful sisters, probably the most famous female threesome in town. The oldest sister, Randy, was Miss Montgomery County. Ruby was a cheerleader at Stewart Junior High. And the youngest, Roberta, called Bobbi, was in fifth grade, a year behind me, at Hartranft.

The Garber girls' father, Bill, was a car salesman on Markley Street, by the brewery. When I was in eighth grade, he sold us our first car, a turtle-green 1952 Pontiac.

Bobbi was a spitfire tomboy. We rode bikes around

the West End. We played in the street. And each school day at noon when classes let out for lunch, Bobbi waited with me at an alley that fed onto Chain Street half a block from school, next to Susan Davis's father's fish market. I was a lieutenant in the safety patrol, and it was my duty to stand at the alley and insure that the kids going home for lunch crossed it safely. I wore a white military-looking strap that circled my waist and looped up diagonally over one shoulder. Pinned to it was my badge, fancy silvered tin with an oval insert painted bright red. I guess I'll never know which dazzled Bobbi more, me or the badge.

I never gave Bobbi Garber a kiss, but I did give her something much more serious, as meaningful a token of my affection as I could manage, and frankly, a fairly painful sacrifice. I gave her my yo-yo. I have since wondered if I truly gave it as a token of affection, or was I finally getting rid of those infernal knots? Whatever, the romance dissolved when I went off to junior high. I never got my yo-yo back.

In seventh grade I moved on to the next level of kissing: lip to lip (or to be precise, teeth to teeth). Until then I had never kissed a female, not even my mother, on the lips, unless you count a few times when our dog Lucky surprised me with a wet one.

This innocent era came to a close on a spring evening in my thirteenth year. I was riding my bike after dinner. There were several hours of daylight left. I was cruising Haws Avenue. I had just made my daily pass of Dovie Wilmoth's house and had crossed Oak into the next block of Haws when I saw several classmates on the sidewalk in front of Kathy Heller's house. They called. I stopped.

Someone said, "Want to play?"

"What?" I said.

"Truth or consequences."

"Okay," I said.

Kathy was there. And Judy Pierson. And Kenny Hengen. And another girl. Apparently they were short on boys.

However the truth part of the game went, the consequence was always the same: You had to kiss a girl. I saw Kenny Hengen do it and thought, *Uh-oh.* He really got into it. Lip to lip, arms around the girl, eyes closed. The smooch seemed to go on for hours, right there on the sidewalk, broad daylight. I had stumbled into the big time. Was I ready for it? Why hadn't I just waved and kept on pedaling? I wished I were still a cowboy. Nearby waited my Roadmaster like a patient, faithful horse.

And then it was my turn. And there was blond-haired Kathy Heller, to whom I hardly ever spoke, with whom I had absolutely nothing in common, standing in front of me, taking off her glasses, awaiting her consequence. Had I time to practice, I might have rehearsed with a pillow or teddy bear. As it was, my lip-eye coordination was a trifle off. I did not so much kiss her as smash my face into hers. Our teeth met with an audible *clack*. But I stayed with it, and so did she. We disengaged teeth and backed off to lip depth and resumed blotting each other. I forgot to close my eyes, however, and to this day I have never had a better view of two eyebrows. When it seemed a respectable amount of time had elapsed, we stopped.

The kiss itself could not have lasted more than three or four seconds, but in my ruminations later it went on for weeks. I soon began to imagine that I had been as bold, smooth, and masterful as Kenny Hengen. Once or twice I heard my Roadmaster whinny, but it was only in my dreams.

When I Was
King

It was January. Snow lay heaped outside Stewart Junior
High School in the far West End of Norristown. Home-
rooms had dismissed an hour before, but dozens of ninth
graders still milled about in the gym. Earlier that day we had
voted for class officers, and we were waiting for the results.

I had run for class president, along with Bill Steinberg, Susan Lane, and Bob Peterson. A teacher came in
and made the announcement. I had won. My old pal
Roger Adelman had won, too; he was vice president.

I'm the second from the left, the newly elected class president of Stewart
Junior High School. In the center is Roger Adelman, my friend and vice president.

I was happy, but I was also uncomfortable. The three other presidential contenders were my friends. In sixth grade Bill Steinberg had finished second to me in the grade-school fifty-yard dash. Now he was my best friend, and here he was trailing me to the finish line again. I apologized to him, he congratulated me, and I think we both took solace in knowing that he was already student council president and that he had gotten faster than I and that if we were to race right then, he would win.

Susan Lane and I had a close, nonkissing kind of relationship. We told each other things we told no one else. We appointed ourselves honorary brother and sister. We trusted each other. Once when a boy asked Susan for a date, she excused herself, hurried to a phone, and called me to ask if she should accept. When I won the election, I apologized to her, too.

I would have apologized to Bob Peterson as well, but I couldn't find him in the gym.

Once I got the apologies out of the way, I was free to feel good—and not just about winning the election. It seems I had won something else, too.

For several years I had admired Judy Pierson, mostly from afar. She had been in my grade at Hartranft, but she was always in the other class. She was at Kathy Heller's house on the Day of the Clacking Teeth, but I don't recall if I ever served as her consequence. In the early months of ninth grade, she had been Nick Salvatore's girlfriend.

But Nick Salvatore was not a basketball player—and I was—and that led to an interesting coincidence involving the "He's Our Man" cheer. In this cheer, each of five cheerleaders was assigned the name of a starting player—in this case Roger Adelman, Louis Darden, Bob Hopple, Bruce Lindeman, or me. And so it went:

"Roger! Roger!
He's our man!
If he can't do it!
Louis can!"

"Louis! Louis!…" and so on to:

"Team! Team!
They're our men!
If they can't do it!
Nobody can!"

To my delight, it was Judy Pierson who had my name. Often the cheer was performed while we were gathered around the coach during a time-out. To anyone looking at the huddling team, I must have appeared to be listening intently to the coach. As a matter of fact, I was listening to Judy Pierson, her lone girl voice echoing through the gym, calling my name:

"Jerry! Jerry!"

I'm here, I wanted to say. And then I was listening to the bleachers pick it up and roar back at her:

"He's our man!"

And then I was peeking at her, at the arms churning, the orange and blue sweater:

"If he can't do it!"

And I was wondering, was it just dumb luck that she got my name, or had she made sure?

I had been hearing reports that since Christmas she had been less than happy with Nick Salvatore. And now I was in the gym not to play basketball but to accept congratulations for winning the election, and Nick Salvatore was nowhere in sight, and Judy Pierson was.

I walked her home that day, down snow-flanked sidewalks. She wore red mittens. Somewhere along Marshall Street I asked if I could hold her hand. She said yes.

There are few times in a life of which it can be said: Nothing is wrong. The twenty minutes that it took for Judy Pierson and me to walk from school to her house on Kohn Street was one such time. It was as if a train I had been riding had dropped me off at a solitary station, and the next train would not be along for twenty minutes. Gone were the shakes and sways and rattles of the old train, yet to come were the distant rumbling mysteries of the next. In the meantime there was only silence and stillness and a brisk cold white world and a girl who had taken off her mitten so that our hands could touch.

I left her at her house on Kohn Street and walked on. As I approached 718 George Street, I saw that my old girlfriend Judy Brooks was making out on the porch with Bob Peterson. I hoped to get by unnoticed, but they took a breath and saw me.

Bob, knowing that I had stayed after school for the election results, called, "Who won?"

I didn't have the heart to tell him. "I don't know," I said. "I left early."

At home that day, no one but Lucky was there to greet me. She yelped and jumped. Her white-tipped tail wagged so violently that it took her entire hindquarters along with it. Lucky, then, became the first in the family to hear that I had been elected class president—and the only one to hear whom I had walked home with.

Judy Pierson and I were now a couple. Each weekday morning one of us—whoever got there first (usually me)—waited for the other in front of Care's Drug Store, on the corner of Kohn and Marshall, and we walked to school together.

We went to school dances together. The dances were held on Friday nights, about one per month. We slow-danced and jitterbugged to 45-rpm records of Elvis Presley, Bill Haley and the Comets, and Ivory Joe Hunter singing "Since I Met You Baby." Once, my parents were chaperons. I danced with my mother while Judy danced with my father. It was now these dances, not Sunday school, that I saved my best outfits for.

On other Friday nights we walked downtown to the Norris movie theater, where we paid more attention to each other than to the screen. Across the street at the Garrick, Roy Rogers and Gene Autry still rode and yodeled through Saturday matinees, but I was no longer there.

On Saturday nights we walked up to Grace Lutheran Church on Haws Avenue. The church welcomed teenagers into a basement room for Ping-Pong, dancing, and refreshments. We danced to "Love Me Tender" by Elvis, "Gone" by Ferlin Husky, "Boppin' the Blues" by Carl Perkins and "The Great Pretender" by the Platters. The latter was "our song." If it came on while I was playing Ping-Pong with one of the guys, I put down my paddle and met Judy on the dance floor.

As the months went by, Judy Pierson and I took our place with such other high-profile couples as Kenny Hengen and Honey Magen, Judy Brooks and Bob Peterson, Marianne Stagliano and Bobby Ruth. We were "serious." We were "going steady." To prove it, Judy wanted a ring.

In Norristown in 1956, if you were going steady with a girl, you gave her a friendship ring. It was tradition. It was custom. Everybody did it. I balked. I told Judy that just because everybody else did it was no reason why we had to. In fact, I said, maybe it was a reason not to. Let's be uniquely us, I said, not like the crowd.

She didn't pester, she didn't pout. She didn't have to. Little by little the mice of conformity nibbled away at my resolve, until one Saturday morning I visited the jewelry shop on Marshall Street and forked over two dollars for a silvery circle of tiny hearts. Judy was thrilled, and before long I forgot why I had balked in the first place.

Hardly a day went by when Judy did not pass a note to me by way of a mutual friend. I've kept the notes in a large envelope all these years. They are written in pencil on low-grade classroom paper, sometimes lined. Most are folded repeatedly into small cubes. The most interesting exception unrolls like a narrow scroll and it measures exactly fifty-two and three-quarter inches long. Outer wrappings are addressed to JERRY SPINELLI **ONLY** or MR. SHORTSTOP. Warnings to would-be snoopers range from PRIVATE to DO NOT TOUCH UNLESS YOU ARE JERRY S. to HANDS OFF—THIS MEANS **YOU**!!!

The letters close with stacks of P.S.'s and parades of exclamation points and flocks of X's.

If I ever wrote a note to Judy, I don't remember. But

I did write notes to myself. Each morning on a small piece of paper I jotted words to remind me of things to talk about as we walked to school. I slipped the paper into my left—or street-side—pocket. If the conversation dragged as we walked up Marshall, I would pull out my crib sheet and take a quick, well-disguised peek.

As I reread Judy's letters, I discover they are an excellent reminder of who and where I was those many years ago. Phrases, sentences stand out:

> *Good luck this afternoon at the game.*

Almost every note says this or something like it. Games were serious business to me. I seldom got home before five o'clock, as I was always practicing after school. I shared quarterback duties with Bob Peterson on the football team, played guard in basketball, and, of course, shortstop in baseball. Ninth grade was my third year as a varsity starter, and though the curve ball still fooled me, I was as determined as ever to become a major leaguer.

> *I hope you win so you are in a good mood at the movies tonight…If a bad mood is good for your hitting, I hope you have a bad mood, but please get out of it by tomorrow.*

As I said, games were serious business—but not as serious as I led Judy to believe. It is true that I felt that putting on a grim "game face" ennobled me and signified my participation in boy stuff that Judy could only cheer about. God forbid I should play at sports as playfully as Louis Darden. It is also true that whenever we lost a game, I turned sullen and sulky. The hidden truth, however, is that this behavior was largely a show—a show for the benefit of the anti-Louis forces within myself and a show to elicit sympathy and admiration from my girlfriend.

I hope you are not still mad at me.

At first I was surprised at how many of the letters contain this sentence. But now that I think back, I do recall at times being possessive and picky and unreasonable and immature. Which is to say, I remember being fifteen.

Remember when you said you probably spoiled my plans about wearing high heels?

Forty years later I don't remember what I said, but I do remember my problems with high heels. Namely, they made her taller than I. How I envied six-foot two-inch Bobby Ruth, whose girlfriend Marianne Stagliano barely came up to his armpits. Happily for me, Judy was understanding, and if she owned a pair of high heels, she must have worn them only to church or in front of her mirror.

But there was nothing she could do about a side-walk. Each morning on our trek up Marshall Street we came to a half-block stretch where the sidewalk sloped down toward the street, so that Judy, walking on the inside, suddenly became taller than I. I hated that stretch, and until we got through it I tended to drift toward the curb and pick up the pace.

Good luck in writing your speech!

After forty years, I fished it out of an old cardboard box: the valedictory speech I wrote, memorized, and de-livered at our graduation from Stewart Junior High School on June 19, 1956. I read it aloud with an eye on the clock. It took less than three minutes. I was pleased to note that the speech was not embarrassingly pompous or stiff and that it even contained a stab at humor.

If people who were there remember anything at all about me that day, I am sure it is not my speech but my outfit: pink shirt with gold cuff links; jacket whose light brown speckled pattern has always made me think of the eggshell of a wild bird, perhaps quail or pheasant; white hanky peeking out of the upper pocket; cream-white linen pants; snow-white suede shoes—called bucks—with eraser-pink gum soles and heels. And the *pièce de résistance*, the tie: knit, square bottom, the perfect triangle of a double Windsor knot. The color was lemon yellow.

I hope you like me in my green gown.

Though it came last, graduation was not the climactic highlight of the year for me. That distinction belonged to the ninth-grade prom, which took place on a Saturday evening in May in the school gym.

After much deliberation Judy had chosen green—the color of her eyes—for her gown. She looked like a bridesmaid, as did all the girls. The skirt of the gown featured layers of stiff crinoline which, when she sat down, spread out like the wings of a brooding swan. No one could sit within three feet of her.

Judy's note about plans for wearing high heels referred to her prom footwear. She was in a quandary. On the one hand, for this occasion of all occasions, she wanted to wear heels. A girl just did not go to a prom in flats. On the other hand, she did not want to violate the Spinelli Ceiling.

One day she happily announced that she had solved the problem. She had bought a new pair of heels for the prom, but they were not high heels. They were low heels. I had not known there was such a thing. She assured me there was and that she would be wearing them and they would not make her too tall and I should just go and win whatever games I was playing and not worry about it. I worried anyway, and when the big night arrived and I in my white jacket and pink carnation went to call for her and nervously stood beside her in the vestibule of her home on 668 Kohn Street and saw that her green eyes were looking straight into mine, I discovered to my enormous relief that she was right.

But neither the color of the gown nor the height of the heels was the thorniest problem that night. Straps were. Perhaps recalling some unpleasantness from a previous prom, the school administration had decreed that gowns could not be strapless. The totally bare shoulder was forbidden. The month of May crackled with the fury of ninth-grade girls. They protested and pleaded. They enlisted Miss Bosler, our class sponsor, in their cause. They petitioned the office. The office would not back down.

Neither did the girls.

In the golden balmy twilight of May 25, the girls and their dates paraded down a corridor of cheering parents and flashing light bulbs to the main entrance of the school, the only time students ever entered that door. Revealed were not only the girls in their finery but also the extent to which they had stretched the definition of the word "strap." There were the merest strings and strands, filaments a spider would envy. One girl's strap was, literally, a thread from a spool. Another girl used eyeliner to paint straps on herself. There were dreamy wisps invisible from ten feet away, sugary confections that hovered above the bodice like a mist.

Some girls, to be sure, Judy Pierson among them, wore conventional straps. But they did so willingly, for hidden in their purses were scissors. Long before Bill March's band played "Goodnight, Sweetheart" for the last dance, every boy on the floor had a bare shoulder to nuzzle.

> *I'm so happy you're King, I always knew you would be. I'm glad I'm Queen with you.*

Judy Pierson and I did not merely go to the prom—we reigned. An hour into the evening all dancing came to a halt as the band struck up "Pomp and Circumstance." The royal couple and the court gathered on the sideline and began doing the hesitation walk (step right foot, pause, step left foot, pause...) along the midcourt line. The girls did it smoothly and naturally; the boys had had to practice, and still we kept messing up.

Me and Judy Pierson on our thrones, reigning over the ninth-grade prom (1956). Judy Brooks, my girlfriend from grades 1 to 4, is second from the right.

We marched to a raised platform that the prom committee had erected in the space between bleacher sections. Judy and I sat on our thrones while the court fanned out before us. Someone placed a wreath of flowers on Judy's head and a cardboard crown on mine. Raymond Morris, who was in my homeroom, had made it. The ends of the crown were stapled in back to make a circle. The color was sky blue, with glitter sprinkled like stars throughout. While the gym resounded with applause and whistles, a photographer from the *Times Herald* planted himself before us. He did not bow to the king and queen, but he did take a picture, which appeared in the paper the following week.

You will always be my King!!!

Johnson Highway

Lucky was dead.

As my brother and I stood over her, breathing hard from our dash to Johnson Highway, I wished I could believe otherwise. She lay in the street near the sidewalk. There was no blood. Her chest and paws were snowy white in the Sunday-afternoon light. But her eyes were open, she did not move, and I could not bring myself to touch her.

Lucky had been a house dog. She did not know about streets and cars.

I could feel Bill's eyes pleading. "Is she?"

I nodded.

We turned away and walked home. Bill cried. I held back. A neighbor called city hall about the body.

Lucky and me in better days (1953).

My life, once so tidy, so perfect, was coming apart. In those first two years at Norristown High, it seemed I lost everything I once had.

I was no longer the big-shot ninth grader in junior high. I was a nobody tenth grader in high school.

I lost my girlfriend not long after she lost the ring of tiny hearts. Her final note said: "Everyone should get away from each other for awhile."

I lost my leadership in the classroom. Whereas I had been a ninth-grade whiz at algebra, geometry in tenth grade befuddled me.

I lost the election for class president.

I lost Louis Darden, my friend and defender. I looked around one day and he was gone.

I lost my dream of becoming a major league baseball player. Though I played a pretty good shortstop for the junior varsity in tenth grade, the following year found me still on the JV's and still unable to hit the curve ball.

I lost my speed. In gym class and team practice races I found myself in the middle of the pack. Once I was even the monkey.

I lost my dog.

And most of all I lost George Street. Halfway through tenth grade we moved to Locust in the North End, where the cellars were called basements, where the furnace was fueled by gas, not coal. Our new home was a brick single-story twin with a driveway beside it for parking the car. It had a yard in front as well as in back. The sidewalk was gleaming concrete.

I lost George Street not only as a location in town but also as a neighborhood in time, a placid side pool of spear fields and black-taped baseballs, of Lash La Rue and grandstand cheers and Roadmaster roamings, a ten-year-long moment that gave me my sense of myself and the world around me. And then the rush of minutes was upon me and I was swept downstream. Instinctively I listened for Mrs. Seeton's whistle, but it did not reach the North End.

Bleak. Dismal. Dreary. Gray. These are the words that come to mind when I think of that time. In fact, the only sunny day I recall was the one on which Lucky died. I do not mean to say that I gave up. I went out for sports, did my homework, went to school dances with the guys. I got my driver's license. I was still just as friendly as I had been a year before, just as neat, just as earnest. But whereas life had once responded by making me king and valedictorian and president, now I was getting election condolences and C's in geometry. Life, like my girlfriend, had dumped me. My string was nothing but knots.

I visited George Street, trying to feel again how it had been. I rode past Dovie Wilmoth's house on Haws Avenue, this time in the family's turtle-green Pontiac. I walked along the railroad tracks humming "Pomp and Circumstance," doing the hesitation step. In my bedroom I touched the cardboard prom crown, now hanging from a corner of my dresser mirror.

When I looked up at night, I discovered that the stars over Locust Street were in the same places as they had been over George, only now they seemed even farther away. They did not inspire me to think of endlessnesses of time and space, they did not make me swoon. They simply made me feel little and lost. Late one night, still awake, I saw tiny sparkles in the dark, as if the starry sky had fallen into my bedroom. It took a minute to realize that I was seeing glitter fallen from the prom crown, a sprinkling on the floor by my dresser, invisible during daylight, caught now in the moonbeam streaming through the window.

On Friday evening, October 11, 1957, at Roosevelt Field, site of my fifty-yard-dash triumph five years before, Norristown High School played Lower Merion in a football game under the lights. Lower Merion was a powerhouse. Over the preceding three years they had won thirty-two games in a row. But Norristown was good, too. It figured to be a close, fiercely contested game, and it was. I was a junior now, sixteen years old, and my autumn sport had become soccer, but I still loved football. I was one of thousands in the grandstand.

As the teams changed field direction for the start

of the fourth quarter, Norristown was leading, 7–6. Each team had scored a touchdown, but the Aces of Lower Merion had missed the extra point. But now a Lower Merion halfback was breaking free and racing downfield, blue-and-white-shirted Norristown Eagles in pursuit. The Eagles stopped him on the one-yard line, and the stage was set for one of the great moments in Norristown's scholastic sports history.

First down and goal to go on the one. One little yard. Thirty-six little inches. Lower Merion. Thirty-two straight victories. Who could stop them? In the bleachers across the field the Lower Merion fans celebrated. Norristown fans grimly awaited the inevitable.

The first Ace ball carrier plunged ahead helmet-first, the Lower Merion side erupted in a touchdown roar—but, strangely, no touchdown sign came from the referee. The ball carrier was crumpled in the rude arms of Eagle defender Mike Branca. The ball had advanced nary an inch.

Twice more the Aces ran the ball, attacking different points in the Eagle defense. The results were the same. The sound from the Lower Merion side was rising and falling as if directed by a choirmaster. But now, as the Ace quarterback bent over the center for the fourth time and barked out the count, Roosevelt Field fell silent. For the fourth time the Ace quarterback handed the ball to a running back—they refused to believe anyone could stop them from ramrodding the ball thirty-six little inches—and for the fourth time the ball failed to penetrate the end zone.

The impossible had been done.

Now it was the Norristown side that erupted, with a roar and a celebration that continued through the end of the game and burst from the stadium and spread out across the town and late into the night. I rode the tide. Lower Merion! We had beaten *Lower Merion!* I couldn't believe it. At home in my room I could hear the blaring horns, the shrieks of victory.

Again and again, following my old habit, I replayed the miraculous Eagle goal-line defense in my head. I went to sleep re-experiencing the event, re-feeling the thrill. In the morning I woke up and daydreamed on— and began to realize that I had a problem. For no matter how many times I replayed the goal-line stand in my head, I kept falling short of satisfaction. The scoreboard had said the game was over, but for me it wasn't, for me it was somehow frustratingly incomplete. I discovered that Roosevelt Field was not the only field that the game had been played on; the other was inside myself. The game kept happening and happening within me. I could not come to the end of it.

And then for no reason that I can recall, I sat down at my study desk and reached for a pencil and paper and wrote down a title. Then I began to write rhyming verses. And the verses became a poem:

Goal to Go

The score stood 7–6
With but five minutes left to go.
The Ace attack employed all tricks
To settle down its stubborn foe.

It looked as though the game was done
When an Ace stepped wide 'round right.
An Eagle stopped him on the one
And tumult filled the night.

Thirty-two had come their way
And thirty-two had died.
Would number thirty-three this day
For one yard be denied?

Roy Kent, the Eagle mentor, said,
"I've waited for this game,
And now, defense, go, stop 'em dead,
And crash the Hall of Fame!"

The first Ace bolted for the goal
And nothing did he see
But Branca, swearing on his soul,
"You shall not pass by me."

The next two plays convinced all
The ref would make the touchdown sign,
But when the light shone on the ball
It still lay inches from the line.

Said Captain Eastwood to his gents,
"It's up to us to stop this drive."
Said Duckworth, Avery, Knerr, and Spence,
"Will do, as long as we're alive."

The halfback drove with all his might,
His legs were jet-propelled,
But when the dust had cleared the fight,
The Eagle line had held.

At last, for me, the game was over.

Fargo, North Dakota

On a September day in 1992, thirty-five years after Norristown High's historic goal-line stand, I stood before an audience of children and adults in Fargo, North Dakota. I was there in connection with my novel *Maniac Magee*, which had recently won the Newbery Medal for children's literature. The important award on this day, however, was the Flicker Tale, which had been voted to *Maniac Magee* as a favorite of North Dakota's young readers. A hundred elementary-school kids sat cross-legged on the floor as I accepted the plaque.

After giving a little talk, I invited the audience to ask questions. There were many. One of them stays with me still. It came from a boy, who said, "Do you think being a kid helped you to become a writer?"

Good question.

After writing "Goal to Go," I gave it to my father and forgot about it. Several days later I opened the *Times Herald* to the sports section, and there was my poem, printed in a box with the headline "Student Waxes Poetic." At school the next day everyone—kids, teachers, football coaches—told me how much they liked it.

That, I believe, was the beginning. By the time I went off to Gettysburg College two years later, I knew I wanted to be a writer.

I graduated from Gettysburg, attended the Writing Seminars at the Johns Hopkins University, spent six months on active duty with the Naval Air Reserve, got a job as a menswear editor for a department store magazine, and in my spare time began to write my first novel.

Three years later I finished it, but no one wanted to publish it. So I wrote another.

And another.

And another.

Wrote them on my lunch hours, after work, weekends. Four novels over thirteen years.

Nobody wanted them.

In the meantime I gained a wife, Eileen, also a writer, and six kids. One day for dinner we had fried chicken. There were leftovers. I packed the unclaimed pieces into a paper bag and put it in the refrigerator, intending to take it to work for lunch the following day. But when I opened the bag early the next morning, I found only chicken bones. The meat had been eaten away.

No doubt this was the work of one of the six little angels sleeping upstairs. Knowing no one would confess (I'm still waiting), I went to work that day lunchless and began to imagine how it might have gone had I known who the culprit was and confronted him or her in the kitchen. By noon I decided to write down my imaginings. I was about to do so, intending to describe the scene from the point of view of the chicken-deprived father, when it suddenly occurred to me that there was a more interesting point of view here—namely, the kid's.

And so with ballpoint pen and yellow copy paper in a tiny windowless office on the fifth floor of the Chilton Company in Radnor, Pennsylvania, I wrote these words:

> *One by one my stepfather took the chicken bones out of the bag and laid them on the kitchen table. He laid them down real neat. In a row. Five of them. Two leg bones, two wing bones, one thigh bone.*
>
> *And bones is all they were. There wasn't a speck of meat on them.*
>
> *Was this really happening? Did my stepfather really drag me out of bed at seven o'clock in the morning on my summer vacation so I could stand in the kitchen in my underpants and stare down at a row of chicken bones?*

That night at home I kept writing. I gave the chicken snatcher a name, Jason, and an age, twelve. And I started remembering. Remembering when I was twelve, when I lived in the West End, when I went to Stewart Junior High School, when I wanted to be a shortstop, when I rode a bike, when I marveled at the nighttime sky. In my head I replayed moments from my kidhood. I mixed my memories with imagination to make stories, to make fiction, and when I finished writing, I had a book, my fifth novel, my first about kids. I called it *Space Station Seventh Grade*.

It became my first published book.

In the years that followed, I continued to write stories about kids and to rummage through the attic of my memories. Norristown became Two Mills in my fiction, George Street became Oriole. There is a prom in one book and a girlfriend named Judy in another. There is a beautiful blonde who lives on an avenue called Haws and a mysterious man on whose front steps no kid dares sit. There is a zep and a mulberry tree, a Little League field, a park, a zoo, a band shell, a red hill, and a mother who whistles her kids home to dinner. There is a river called Schuylkill and a creek called Stony and a grocery store on a corner next to a house whose address is 802. And a brown finger in a white mouth. And a boy who is a wizard at untying knots in yo-yo strings.

Do you think being a kid helped you to become a writer?

I could have taken days to answer the boy's question, but neither he nor Fargo had that much time. So I simply nodded and smiled and said, "Yes, I believe it did."

Books by Jerry Spinelli

About the Author

Jerry Spinelli is the author of many books for young readers, including *Maniac Magee*, winner of the Newbery Medal; *Wringer*, winner of a Newbery Honor Award; *Loser*; *Crash*; and *Stargirl*. A graduate of Gettysburg College, he lives in Pennsylvania with his wife, poet and author Eileen Spinelli.

Jerry Spinelli, age 11   Jerry Spinelli, today